HARCOURT

Math

Practice
Workbook

PUPIL EDITION
Grade 1

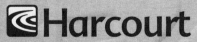

Harcourt

Orlando • Boston • Dallas • Chicago • San Diego
www.harcourtschool.com

ISBN 0-15-320435-4

15 073 09 08 07

CONTENTS

Addition Stories

Use ● to show an addition story.

Draw the ●.

Write the numbers.

1.

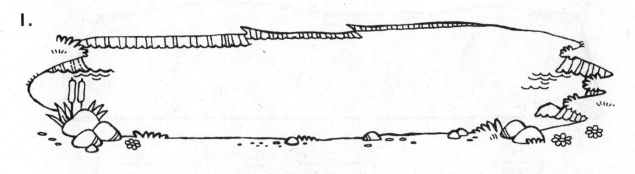

_____ ducks   _____ ducks come   _____ in all

2.

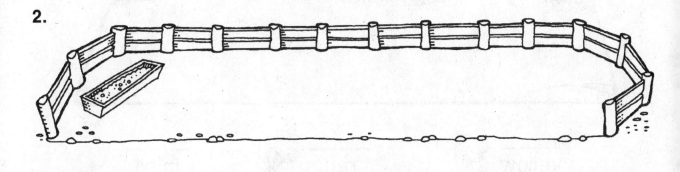

_____ pigs   _____ pigs come   _____ in all

 Mixed Review

Write the missing numbers.

3. 2, 3, _____

4. 7, 8, _____

5. 3, _____, 5

6. _____, 3, 4

More Addition Stories

Use ● to show an addition story.

Draw the ●. Write the numbers.

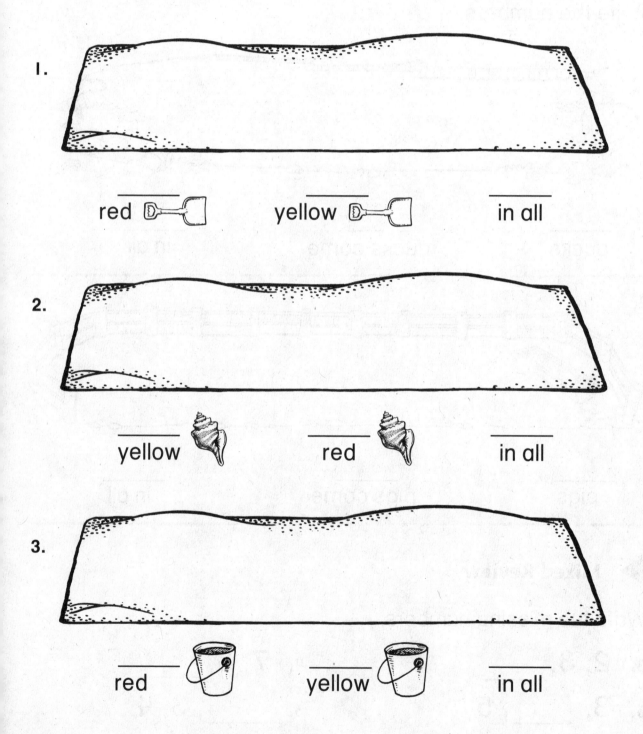

1.

_____ red 🔨   _____ yellow 🔨   _____ in all

2.

_____ yellow 🐚   _____ red 🐚   _____ in all

3.

_____ red 🪣   _____ yellow 🪣   _____ in all

Add with Pictures

Add. Write the sum.

1.

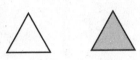

$$1 \ + \ 1 \ = \ \underline{2}$$

2.

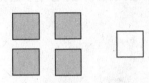

$$4 \ + \ 1 \ = \ \underline{}$$

3.

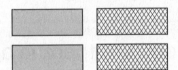

$$2 \ + \ 2 \ = \ \underline{}$$

4.

$$4 \ + \ 2 \ = \ \underline{}$$

5.

$$3 \ + \ 2 \ = \ \underline{}$$

6.

$$2 \ + \ 1 \ = \ \underline{}$$

▶ **Mixed Review**

Write the number that is between.

7. 7, _____, 9   8. 3, _____, 5   9. 6, _____, 8

10. 5, _____, 7   11. 8, _____, 10   12. 4, _____, 6

Problem Solving • Write an Addition Sentence

Write the addition sentence.

1. How many are there in all?

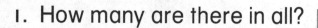

_4_ ⊕ _2_ ⊖ _6_

2. How many are there in all?

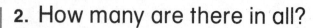

___ ◯ ___ ◯ ___

3. How many are there in all?

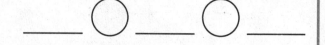

___ ◯ ___ ◯ ___

4. How many are there in all?

___ ◯ ___ ◯ ___

5. How many are there in all?

___ ◯ ___ ◯ ___

6. How many are there in all?

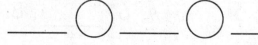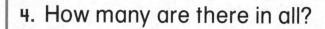

___ ◯ ___ ◯ ___

Add 0

Draw circles to show each number.
Write the sum.

1.

⊙ | ⊙ ⊙⊙ | ⊙ ⊙⊙⊙

| 1 + 0 = ___ | 1 + 2 = ___ | 1 + 3 = ___ |

2.

| 3 + 0 = ___ | 3 + 3 = ___ | 3 + 2 = ___ |

3.

| 4 + 1 = ___ | 4 + 0 = ___ | 4 + 2 = ___ |

4.

| 2 + 1 = ___ | 2 + 2 = ___ | 2 + 0 = ___ |

▶ **Mixed Review**

Write the number that comes next.

5. 3, 4, 5, ____   6. 5, 4, 3, ____

7. 4, 3, 2, ____   8. 6, 5, 4, ____

Add in Any Order

Use  and ⬛ to add.
Circle the two addition sentences
that have the same sum.

1. $2 + 1 = \underline{3}$ $1 + 0 = \underline{1}$ $1 + 2 = \underline{3}$

2. $0 + 3 = \underline{}$ $3 + 1 = \underline{}$ $1 + 3 = \underline{}$

3. $2 + 4 = \underline{}$ $4 + 1 = \underline{}$ $4 + 2 = \underline{}$

4. $0 + 1 = \underline{}$ $4 + 0 = \underline{}$ $0 + 4 = \underline{}$

5. $3 + 2 = \underline{}$ $2 + 3 = \underline{}$ $2 + 0 = \underline{}$

6. $5 + 1 = \underline{}$ $1 + 5 = \underline{}$ $3 + 3 = \underline{}$

▶ **Mixed Review**

Circle the greater number.

7. 9 or 8   **8.** 4 or 7   **9.** 10 or 11

10. 5 or 7   **11.** 6 or 3   **12.** 12 or 10

Name _____

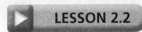

Ways to Make 7 and 8

Use 🎲 and 🎲 to make 7.
Color. Write the addition sentence.

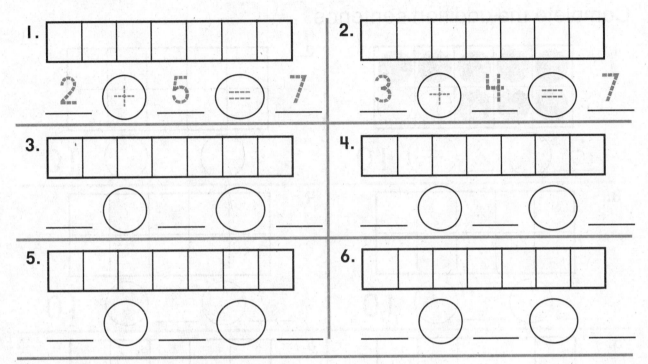

1.
2.

$2 + 5 = 7$ $3 + 4 = 7$

___ (+) ___ (=) ___   ___ (+) ___ (=) ___

3.
4.

___ ◯ ___ ◯ ___   ___ ◯ ___ ◯ ___

5.
6.

___ ◯ ___ ◯ ___   ___ ◯ ___ ◯ ___

Use 🎲 and 🎲 to make 8.
Color. Write the addition sentence.

7.
8.

___ ◯ ___ ◯ ___   ___ ◯ ___ ◯ ___

9.
10.

___ ◯ ___ ◯ ___   ___ ◯ ___ ◯ ___

11.
12.

___ ◯ ___ ◯ ___   ___ ◯ ___ ◯ ___

Ways to Make 9 and 10

Use Workmat 7, ●, and ○
to make 9 or 10. Draw and color.
Complete the addition sentence.

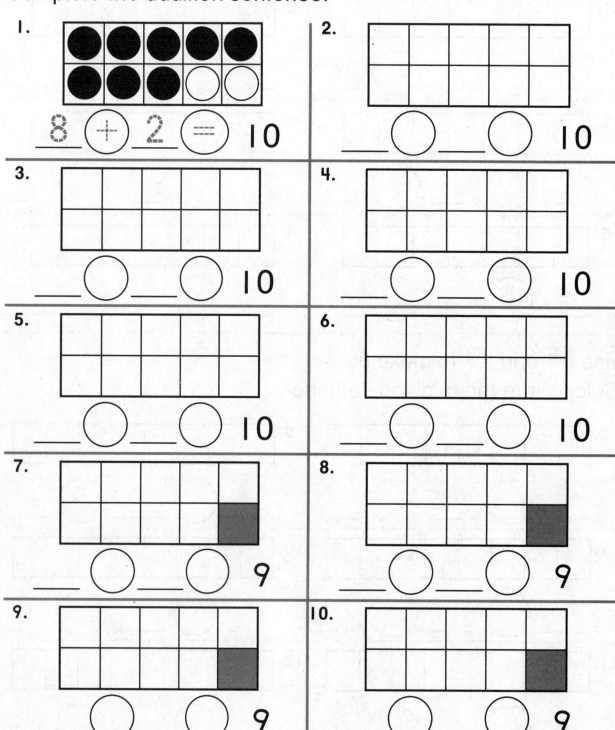

1. _8_ ⊕ _2_ ⊜ 10

2. ___ ◯ ___ ◯ 10

3. ___ ◯ ___ ◯ 10

4. ___ ◯ ___ ◯ 10

5. ___ ◯ ___ ◯ 10

6. ___ ◯ ___ ◯ 10

7. ___ ◯ ___ ◯ 9

8. ___ ◯ ___ ◯ 9

9. ___ ◯ ___ ◯ 9

10. ___ ◯ ___ ◯ 9

Count On 1 and 2

Use ● . Count on to find the sum.

1. $7 + 2 = \underline{9}$ | 2. $6 + 1 = \underline{7}$

3. $4 + 2 = \underline{}$ $5 + 1 = \underline{}$ $8 + 2 = \underline{}$

4. $2 + 2 = \underline{}$ $1 + 2 = \underline{}$ $8 + 1 = \underline{}$

5. $5 + 2 = \underline{}$ $3 + 1 = \underline{}$ $7 + 1 = \underline{}$

6. $6 + 2 = \underline{}$ $4 + 1 = \underline{}$ $3 + 2 = \underline{}$

▶ **Mixed Review**

Write the number that is one more.

7. 6, _____   4, _____   2, _____

8. 5, _____   7, _____   9, _____

Count On 1, 2, and 3

Count on to find the sum.

1.
$$
\begin{array}{r} 6 \\ +\ 3 \\ \hline 9 \end{array}
$$

Say 6.
Count on 3.
7,8,9

$$
\begin{array}{r} 3 \\ +\ 2 \\ \hline \end{array}
$$

$$
\begin{array}{r} 4 \\ +\ 1 \\ \hline \end{array}
$$

$$
\begin{array}{r} 5 \\ +\ 2 \\ \hline \end{array}
$$

2.
$$
\begin{array}{r} 7 \\ +\ 3 \\ \hline \end{array}
$$

$$
\begin{array}{r} 6 \\ +\ 2 \\ \hline \end{array}
$$

$$
\begin{array}{r} 3 \\ +\ 3 \\ \hline \end{array}
$$

$$
\begin{array}{r} 6 \\ +\ 1 \\ \hline \end{array}
$$

$$
\begin{array}{r} 1 \\ +\ 2 \\ \hline \end{array}
$$

3.
$$
\begin{array}{r} 4 \\ +\ 3 \\ \hline \end{array}
$$

$$
\begin{array}{r} 4 \\ +\ 2 \\ \hline \end{array}
$$

$$
\begin{array}{r} 2 \\ +\ 2 \\ \hline \end{array}
$$

$$
\begin{array}{r} 5 \\ +\ 1 \\ \hline \end{array}
$$

$$
\begin{array}{r} 7 \\ +\ 1 \\ \hline \end{array}
$$

4.
$$
\begin{array}{r} 8 \\ +\ 2 \\ \hline \end{array}
$$

$$
\begin{array}{r} 5 \\ +\ 3 \\ \hline \end{array}
$$

$$
\begin{array}{r} 2 \\ +\ 1 \\ \hline \end{array}
$$

$$
\begin{array}{r} 8 \\ +\ 1 \\ \hline \end{array}
$$

$$
\begin{array}{r} 7 \\ +\ 2 \\ \hline \end{array}
$$

▶ **Mixed Review**

Write the missing number.

5. 2, 3, ____, 5

6. 7, 8, 9, ____

7. ____, 5, 6, 7

8. 3, 4, ____, 6, 7

Doubles

Circle the doubles facts.
Then add.

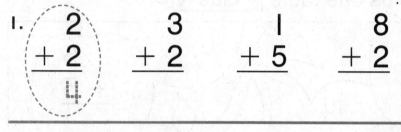

1.
$$\begin{array}{r} 2 \\ + 2 \\ \hline 4 \end{array}\qquad \begin{array}{r} 3 \\ + 2 \\ \hline \end{array}\qquad \begin{array}{r} 1 \\ + 5 \\ \hline \end{array}\qquad \begin{array}{r} 8 \\ + 2 \\ \hline \end{array}\qquad \begin{array}{r} 4 \\ + 2 \\ \hline \end{array}\qquad \begin{array}{r} 0 \\ + 0 \\ \hline \end{array}$$

2.
$$\begin{array}{r} 9 \\ + 1 \\ \hline \end{array}\qquad \begin{array}{r} 7 \\ + 3 \\ \hline \end{array}\qquad \begin{array}{r} 1 \\ + 9 \\ \hline \end{array}\qquad \begin{array}{r} 2 \\ + 6 \\ \hline \end{array}\qquad \begin{array}{r} 5 \\ + 5 \\ \hline \end{array}\qquad \begin{array}{r} 7 \\ + 1 \\ \hline \end{array}$$

3.
$$\begin{array}{r} 5 \\ + 2 \\ \hline \end{array}\qquad \begin{array}{r} 1 \\ + 1 \\ \hline \end{array}\qquad \begin{array}{r} 7 \\ + 2 \\ \hline \end{array}\qquad \begin{array}{r} 4 \\ + 1 \\ \hline \end{array}\qquad \begin{array}{r} 1 \\ + 2 \\ \hline \end{array}\qquad \begin{array}{r} 4 \\ + 3 \\ \hline \end{array}$$

4.
$$\begin{array}{r} 5 \\ + 3 \\ \hline \end{array}\qquad \begin{array}{r} 8 \\ + 1 \\ \hline \end{array}\qquad \begin{array}{r} 4 \\ + 0 \\ \hline \end{array}\qquad \begin{array}{r} 3 \\ + 3 \\ \hline \end{array}\qquad \begin{array}{r} 1 \\ + 6 \\ \hline \end{array}\qquad \begin{array}{r} 4 \\ + 4 \\ \hline \end{array}$$

▶ **Mixed Review**

Solve.

5. $3 + 2 =$ _____ $5 + 2 =$ _____ $6 + 1 =$ _____

6. $4 - 3 =$ _____ $7 - 2 =$ _____ $4 - 2 =$ _____

Doubles Plus 1

1. Add. Color the doubles facts **yellow** 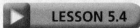.

   Color the doubles plus one facts **blue** ▷.

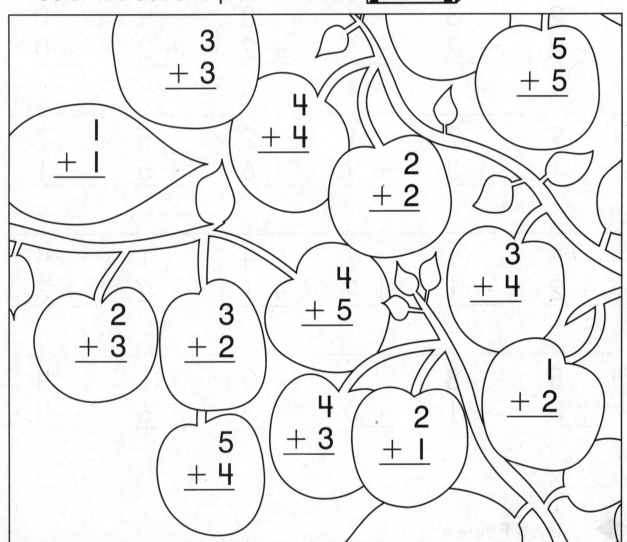

▶ **Mixed Review**

Write the sum or difference.

2. $7 - 2 =$ _____ $3 + 2 =$ _____ $3 - 1 =$ _____

Problem Solving • Draw a Picture

Draw a picture to solve.
Write an addition sentence to check.

1. 3 puppies jump.
   4 puppies sleep.
   How many puppies are there?

   ___3___ ⊕ ___4___ ⊜ ___7___

   ___7___ puppies

2. There are 2 trees.
   There are 4 birds on each tree.
   How many birds are there?

   _____ ◯ _____ ◯ _____

   _____ birds

3. There are 7 frogs on a log.
   3 more frogs come.
   How many frogs are there?

   _____ ◯ _____ ◯ _____

   _____ frogs

4. 5 mice run.
   3 mice sit.
   How many are there in all?

   _____ ◯ _____ ◯ _____

   _____ mice

Remember the Facts

Circle all the doubles. Then add. Write the sum.

1.
$$\begin{array}{r} 4 \\ + 3 \\ \hline 7 \end{array} \qquad \begin{array}{r} 2 \\ + 3 \\ \hline \end{array} \qquad \begin{array}{r} 3 \\ + 3 \\ \hline \end{array} \qquad \begin{array}{r} 4 \\ + 1 \\ \hline \end{array} \qquad \begin{array}{r} 2 \\ + 4 \\ \hline \end{array}$$

2.
$$\begin{array}{r} 3 \\ + 5 \\ \hline \end{array} \qquad \begin{array}{r} 6 \\ + 4 \\ \hline \end{array} \qquad \begin{array}{r} 7 \\ + 2 \\ \hline \end{array} \qquad \begin{array}{r} 9 \\ + 1 \\ \hline \end{array} \qquad \begin{array}{r} 8 \\ + 2 \\ \hline \end{array}$$

3.
$$\begin{array}{r} 5 \\ + 5 \\ \hline \end{array} \qquad \begin{array}{r} 3 \\ + 4 \\ \hline \end{array} \qquad \begin{array}{r} 3 \\ + 1 \\ \hline \end{array} \qquad \begin{array}{r} 2 \\ + 2 \\ \hline \end{array} \qquad \begin{array}{r} 5 \\ + 2 \\ \hline \end{array}$$

4.
$$\begin{array}{r} 1 \\ + 1 \\ \hline \end{array} \qquad \begin{array}{r} 4 \\ + 4 \\ \hline \end{array} \qquad \begin{array}{r} 1 \\ + 2 \\ \hline \end{array} \qquad \begin{array}{r} 5 \\ + 1 \\ \hline \end{array} \qquad \begin{array}{r} 6 \\ + 2 \\ \hline \end{array}$$

▶ **Mixed Review**

Solve.

5. $5 + 5 = $ _____ $4 + 5 = $ _____ $2 + 6 = $ _____

6. $4 + 2 = $ _____ $7 + 1 = $ _____ $3 + 3 = $ _____

7. $1 + 5 = $ _____ $3 + 5 = $ _____ $4 + 4 = $ _____

Practice Sums Through 8

Add. Use the key.

Color each balloon by its sum.

What pattern do you see?

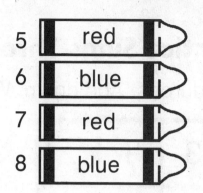

5	red
6	blue
7	red
8	blue

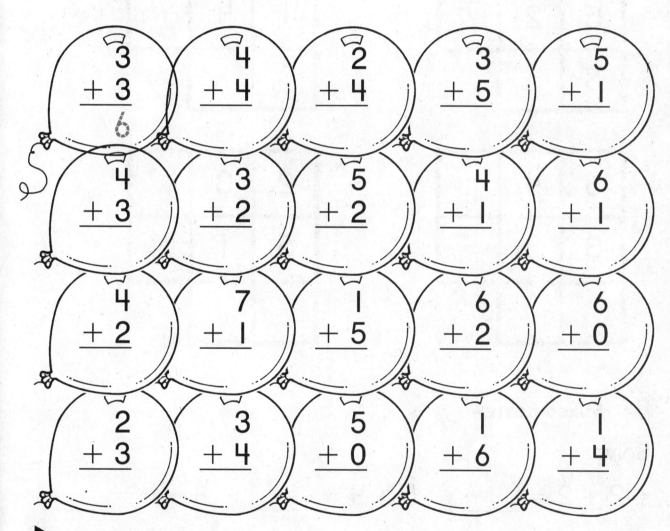

$$\begin{array}{r} 3 \\ +3 \\ \hline 6 \end{array}\quad \begin{array}{r} 4 \\ +4 \\ \hline \end{array}\quad \begin{array}{r} 2 \\ +4 \\ \hline \end{array}\quad \begin{array}{r} 3 \\ +5 \\ \hline \end{array}\quad \begin{array}{r} 5 \\ +1 \\ \hline \end{array}$$

$$\begin{array}{r} 4 \\ +3 \\ \hline \end{array}\quad \begin{array}{r} 3 \\ +2 \\ \hline \end{array}\quad \begin{array}{r} 5 \\ +2 \\ \hline \end{array}\quad \begin{array}{r} 4 \\ +1 \\ \hline \end{array}\quad \begin{array}{r} 6 \\ +1 \\ \hline \end{array}$$

$$\begin{array}{r} 4 \\ +2 \\ \hline \end{array}\quad \begin{array}{r} 7 \\ +1 \\ \hline \end{array}\quad \begin{array}{r} 1 \\ +5 \\ \hline \end{array}\quad \begin{array}{r} 6 \\ +2 \\ \hline \end{array}\quad \begin{array}{r} 6 \\ +0 \\ \hline \end{array}$$

$$\begin{array}{r} 2 \\ +3 \\ \hline \end{array}\quad \begin{array}{r} 3 \\ +4 \\ \hline \end{array}\quad \begin{array}{r} 5 \\ +0 \\ \hline \end{array}\quad \begin{array}{r} 1 \\ +6 \\ \hline \end{array}\quad \begin{array}{r} 1 \\ +4 \\ \hline \end{array}$$

▶ **Mixed Review**

Solve.

1. $2 + 2 =$ _____ $2 + 1 =$ _____ $3 + 3 =$ _____

2. $7 + 0 =$ _____ $1 + 1 =$ _____ $3 + 1 =$ _____

Name _____

Practice Sums Through 10

Add across. Add down. Write the sums.

1.
3	4	7
5	2	7
8	6	

2.
8	2	
1	4	

3.
6	4	
3	3	

4.
2	3	
5	1	

▶ **Mixed Review**

Solve.

5. 2 + 2 = ____   5 + 4 = ____   4 + 4 = ____

6. 6 + 2 = ____   3 + 4 = ____   4 + 5 = ____

7. 1 + 6 = ____   0 + 5 = ____   7 + 3 = ____

Algebra • Follow the Rule

Complete the table.
Follow the rule.

1.

Add 1	
6	7
7	8
8	9

2.

Add 6	
1	
2	
3	

3.

Add 5	
2	
3	
4	

4.

Add 2	
2	
4	
6	

5.

Add 4	
1	
3	
5	

6.

Add 3	
3	
4	
5	

▶ **Mixed Review**

Solve.

7. $3 + 2 =$ _____ $4 + 4 =$ _____ $2 + 1 =$ _____

8. $1 + 8 =$ _____ $6 + 3 =$ _____ $2 + 2 =$ _____

9. $1 + 1 =$ _____ $5 + 2 =$ _____ $4 + 5 =$ _____

Problem Solving • Write a Number Sentence

Solve. Write a number sentence.
Draw a picture to check.

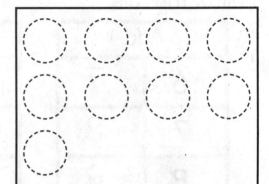

1. 5 ducks are in a pond.
   4 more come.
   How many ducks are there?

   __5__ (+) __4__ (=) __9__ ducks

2. 3 goats are on the hill.
   4 goats are in the field.
   How many goats are there?

   ____ ◯ ____ ◯ ____ goats

3. There are 7 white rabbits.
   There are 3 brown rabbits.
   How many rabbits are there?

   ____ ◯ ____ ◯ ____ rabbits

4. There are 4 deer.
   4 more come.
   How many deer are there?

   ____ ◯ ____ ◯ ____ deer

Count Back 1 and 2

Use the number line.
Count back to subtract.

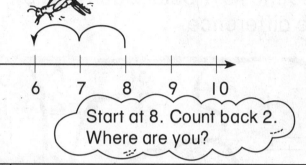

1.

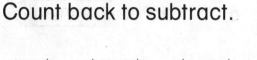

$$8 - 2 = \underline{6}$$

Start at 8. Count back 2.
Where are you?

2.

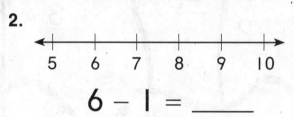

$$6 - 1 = \underline{}$$

3.

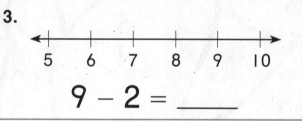

$$9 - 2 = \underline{}$$

4.

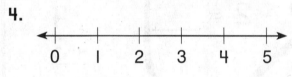

$$2 - 2 = \underline{}$$

5.

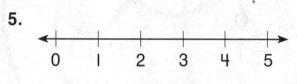

$$5 - 2 = \underline{}$$

6.

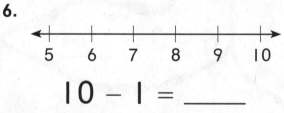

$$10 - 1 = \underline{}$$

7.

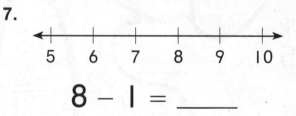

$$8 - 1 = \underline{}$$

▶ **Mixed Review**

Solve.

8. $2 + 3 = \underline{}$ $4 + 2 = \underline{}$ $2 + 2 = \underline{}$

9. $6 + 3 = \underline{}$ $5 + 5 = \underline{}$ $7 + 1 = \underline{}$

10. $2 + 1 = \underline{}$ $6 + 2 = \underline{}$ $5 + 3 = \underline{}$

Name _____

Count Back 3

Count back to subtract.
Use the key. Color each part by the difference.

5 or less 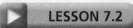 green

6 or greater orange

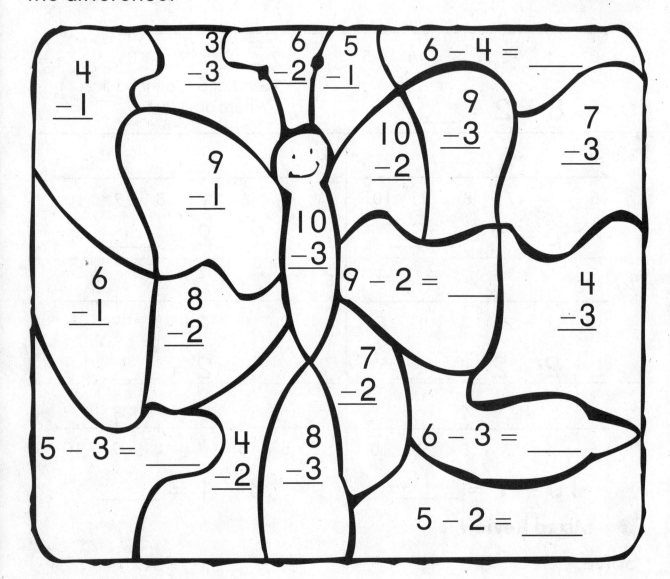

Inside the coloring puzzle:

$4 - 1$

$3 - 3$

$6 - 2$

$5 - 1$

$6 - 4 =$ ___

$9 - 3$

$10 - 2$

$7 - 3$

$9 - 1$

$10 - 3$

$9 - 2 =$ ___

$4 - 3$

$6 - 1$

$8 - 2$

$7 - 2$

$5 - 3 =$ ___

$4 - 2$

$8 - 3$

$6 - 3 =$ ___

$5 - 2 =$ ___

▶ **Mixed Review**

Solve.

1. $2 + 3 =$ ___ $5 + 5 =$ ___ $7 + 2 =$ ___

2. $5 + 3 =$ ___ $9 - 2 =$ ___ $4 - 2 =$ ___

PW32 Practice

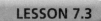

Relate Addition and Subtraction

Add. Then subtract.

1.

$6 + 3 = \underline{9}$

$9 - 3 = \underline{6}$

2.

$8 + 1 = \underline{}$

$9 - 1 = \underline{}$

3.

$6 + 2 = \underline{}$

$8 - 2 = \underline{}$

4.

$3 + 5 = \underline{}$

$8 - 5 = \underline{}$

▶ **Mixed Review**

Solve.

5. $3 + 2 = \underline{}$ $6 + 1 = \underline{}$ $5 - 3 = \underline{}$

6. $8 - 2 = \underline{}$ $9 - 3 = \underline{}$ $7 + 1 = \underline{}$

Problem Solving • Draw a Picture

Draw a picture to solve the problem.
Write how many went inside.

1. There were 7 pigs.
Some pigs went inside
the barn. How many
pigs went inside?

____3____ pigs

2. There were 5 puppies.
Some puppies went inside
the basket. How many
puppies went inside?

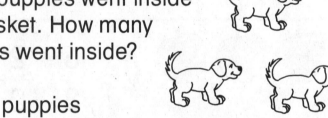

_____ puppies

3. There were 6 bunnies.
Some went inside the house.
How many bunnies
went inside?

_____ bunnies

4. There were 8 frogs.
Some went inside a log.
How many frogs
went inside?

_____ frogs

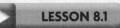

Remember the Facts

Circle the facts for **subtract 0** and for **subtract all**.
Subtract. Write the differences.

1.
$$\begin{array}{r} 5 \\ -\,0 \\ \hline 5 \end{array}$$
$$\begin{array}{r} 6 \\ -\,3 \\ \hline \end{array}$$
$$\begin{array}{r} 7 \\ -\,3 \\ \hline \end{array}$$
$$\begin{array}{r} 8 \\ -\,2 \\ \hline \end{array}$$
$$\begin{array}{r} 9 \\ -\,3 \\ \hline \end{array}$$
$$\begin{array}{r} 10 \\ -\,10 \\ \hline \end{array}$$

2.
$$\begin{array}{r} 5 \\ -\,2 \\ \hline \end{array}$$
$$\begin{array}{r} 9 \\ -\,0 \\ \hline \end{array}$$
$$\begin{array}{r} 7 \\ -\,2 \\ \hline \end{array}$$
$$\begin{array}{r} 7 \\ -\,7 \\ \hline \end{array}$$
$$\begin{array}{r} 9 \\ -\,2 \\ \hline \end{array}$$
$$\begin{array}{r} 5 \\ -\,1 \\ \hline \end{array}$$

3.
$$\begin{array}{r} 10 \\ -\,1 \\ \hline \end{array}$$
$$\begin{array}{r} 6 \\ -\,2 \\ \hline \end{array}$$
$$\begin{array}{r} 8 \\ -\,8 \\ \hline \end{array}$$
$$\begin{array}{r} 8 \\ -\,3 \\ \hline \end{array}$$
$$\begin{array}{r} 6 \\ -\,1 \\ \hline \end{array}$$
$$\begin{array}{r} 10 \\ -\,3 \\ \hline \end{array}$$

4.
$$\begin{array}{r} 10 \\ -\,0 \\ \hline \end{array}$$
$$\begin{array}{r} 9 \\ -\,1 \\ \hline \end{array}$$
$$\begin{array}{r} 8 \\ -\,1 \\ \hline \end{array}$$
$$\begin{array}{r} 7 \\ -\,1 \\ \hline \end{array}$$
$$\begin{array}{r} 6 \\ -\,0 \\ \hline \end{array}$$
$$\begin{array}{r} 10 \\ -\,2 \\ \hline \end{array}$$

▶ **Mixed Review**

Solve.

5. $3 + 2 =$ _____ $4 - 3 =$ _____ $2 + 5 =$ _____

6. $3 + 5 =$ _____ $4 + 4 =$ _____ $4 + 2 =$ _____

Practice Subtraction Through 8

Subtract across. Subtract down.

1.

4	2	2
3	1	2
1	1	0

2.

7	4	
5	4	

3.

6	2	
5	2	

4.

8	3	
7	3	

▶ **Mixed Review**

Use addition to help you subtract.

5. $6 + 3 = 9$ $4 + 4 = 8$ $3 + 2 = 5$

$9 - 3 =$ ___ $8 - 4 =$ ___ $5 - 2 =$ ___

6. $8 + 2 = 10$ $4 + 3 = 7$ $5 + 1 = 6$

$10 - 2 =$ ___ $7 - 3 =$ ___ $6 - 1 =$ ___

Practice Subtraction Through 10

Subtract. Use the key.

Color each part by its difference.

| 4 blue | 7 yellow | 5 purple | 6 orange |

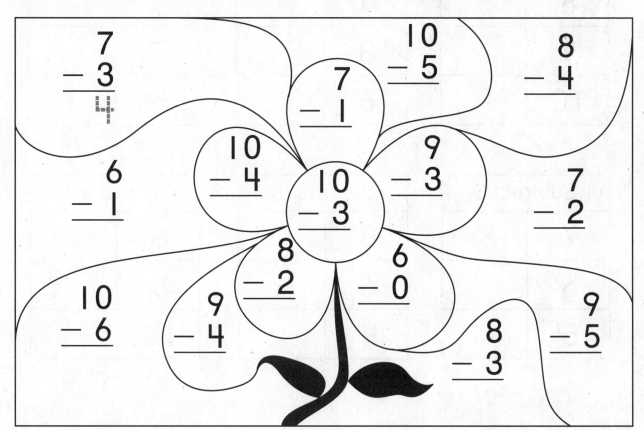

$$\begin{array}{r} 7 \\ -3 \\ \hline 4 \end{array}$$

$$\begin{array}{r} 10 \\ -5 \\ \hline \end{array}$$

$$\begin{array}{r} 8 \\ -4 \\ \hline \end{array}$$

$$\begin{array}{r} 7 \\ -1 \\ \hline \end{array}$$

$$\begin{array}{r} 6 \\ -1 \\ \hline \end{array}$$

$$\begin{array}{r} 10 \\ -4 \\ \hline \end{array}$$

$$\begin{array}{r} 10 \\ -3 \\ \hline \end{array}$$

$$\begin{array}{r} 9 \\ -3 \\ \hline \end{array}$$

$$\begin{array}{r} 7 \\ -2 \\ \hline \end{array}$$

$$\begin{array}{r} 8 \\ -2 \\ \hline \end{array}$$

$$\begin{array}{r} 6 \\ -0 \\ \hline \end{array}$$

$$\begin{array}{r} 10 \\ -6 \\ \hline \end{array}$$

$$\begin{array}{r} 9 \\ -4 \\ \hline \end{array}$$

$$\begin{array}{r} 8 \\ -3 \\ \hline \end{array}$$

$$\begin{array}{r} 9 \\ -5 \\ \hline \end{array}$$

▶ **Mixed Review**

Put a + or − in the circle to make
the number sentence correct.

1. $5 \bigcirc 3 = 8$ $6 \bigcirc 2 = 4$ $7 \bigcirc 3 = 4$

2. $10 \bigcirc 2 = 8$ $4 \bigcirc 5 = 9$ $7 \bigcirc 2 = 5$

3. $8 \bigcirc 2 = 10$ $4 \bigcirc 3 = 1$ $4 \bigcirc 4 = 8$

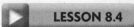

Algebra • Follow the Rule

Complete the table. Follow the rule.

1.

Subtract 2	
8	6
9	7
10	

2.

Subtract 5	
10	
8	
6	

3.

Subtract 4	
9	
7	
5	

4.

Subtract 3	
7	
6	
5	

5.

Subtract 0	
8	
6	
4	

6.

Subtract 1	
6	
8	
10	

▶ **Mixed Review**

Solve.

7. $7 + 2 =$ _____ $3 + 5 =$ _____ $2 + 5 =$ _____

8. $5 - 3 =$ _____ $7 - 5 =$ _____ $9 - 1 =$ _____

9. $6 - 3 =$ _____ $8 - 5 =$ _____ $4 - 2 =$ _____

10. $5 + 5 =$ _____ $6 + 2 =$ _____ $1 + 4 =$ _____

Fact Families

Add or subtract.

Write the numbers in the **fact family.**

1.

$$\begin{array}{r} 4 \\ + 2 \\ \hline 6 \end{array}$$

$$\begin{array}{r} 2 \\ + 4 \\ \hline 6 \end{array}$$

$$\begin{array}{r} 6 \\ - 2 \\ \hline 4 \end{array}$$

$$\begin{array}{r} 6 \\ - 4 \\ \hline 2 \end{array}$$

| 4 | | 2 | | 6 |

2.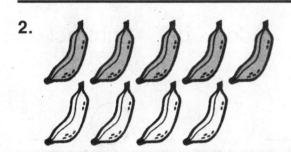

$$\begin{array}{r} 5 \\ + 4 \\ \hline \end{array}$$

$$\begin{array}{r} 4 \\ + 5 \\ \hline \end{array}$$

$$\begin{array}{r} 9 \\ - 4 \\ \hline \end{array}$$

$$\begin{array}{r} 9 \\ - 5 \\ \hline \end{array}$$

| | | | | |

3.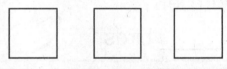

$$\begin{array}{r} 5 \\ + 3 \\ \hline \end{array}$$

$$\begin{array}{r} 3 \\ + 5 \\ \hline \end{array}$$

$$\begin{array}{r} 8 \\ - 3 \\ \hline \end{array}$$

$$\begin{array}{r} 8 \\ - 5 \\ \hline \end{array}$$

| | | | | |

▶ **Mixed Review**

Solve.

4. $1 + 7 =$ _____ $2 + 3 =$ _____ $3 + 4 =$ _____

5. $5 - 4 =$ _____ $8 - 3 =$ _____ $9 - 7 =$ _____

Problem Solving • Choose the Operation

Circle **add** or **subtract**.

Write the number sentence.

1. 6 puppies chew bones.
   3 more come to chew.
   How many puppies are
   there now?

   __9__ puppies

   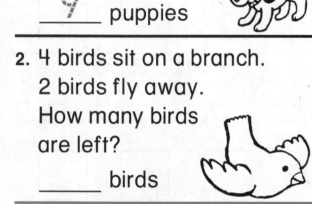

   (Add)   or   Subtract

   6 (+) 3 (=) 9

2. 4 birds sit on a branch.
   2 birds fly away.
   How many birds
   are left?

   _____ birds

   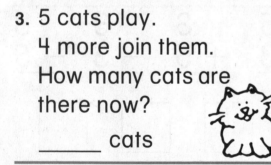

   Add   or   Subtract

   ___ ◯ ___ ◯ ___

3. 5 cats play.
   4 more join them.
   How many cats are
   there now?

   _____ cats

   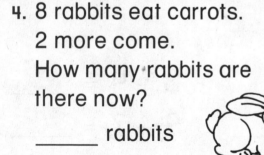

   Add   or   Subtract

   ___ ◯ ___ ◯ ___

4. 8 rabbits eat carrots.
   2 more come.
   How many rabbits are
   there now?

   _____ rabbits

   Add   or   Subtract

   ___ ◯ ___ ◯ ___

Tens

Write how many tens.
Count by tens. Write the number.

1.

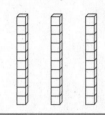

$\dfrac{3}{\text{tens}}$ $\dfrac{30}{\text{thirty}}$

2.

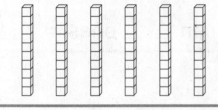

$\dfrac{}{\text{tens}}$ $\dfrac{}{\text{sixty}}$

3.

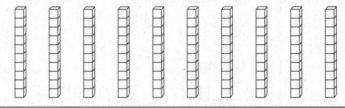

$\dfrac{}{\text{tens}}$ $\dfrac{}{\text{one hundred}}$

4.

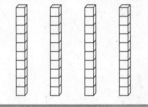

$\dfrac{}{\text{tens}}$ $\dfrac{}{\text{forty}}$

5.

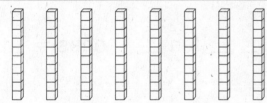

$\dfrac{}{\text{tens}}$ $\dfrac{}{\text{eighty}}$

▶ **Mixed Review**

Solve.

6. $3 + 3 =$ ___ $2 + 3 =$ ___ $4 + 4 =$ ___

7. $5 - 3 =$ ___ $7 - 1 =$ ___ $5 - 1 =$ ___

8. $2 + 4 =$ ___ $4 + 1 =$ ___ $6 + 2 =$ ___

Tens and Ones to 20

Write how many tens and ones.
Write the number.

1.

 1 ten **5** ones = **15**

2.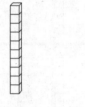

____ ten ____ ones = ____

3.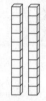

____ tens ____ ones = ____

4.

____ ten ____ ones = ____

5.

____ ten ____ ones = ____

6.

____ ten ____ ones = ____

▶ **Mixed Review**

Solve.

7. $6 - 4 =$ ____ $8 + 2 =$ ____ $7 - 4 =$ ____

8. $9 - 4 =$ ____ $8 + 1 =$ ____ $6 + 3 =$ ____

9. $7 + 2 =$ ____ $5 + 4 =$ ____ $9 - 7 =$ ____

10. $6 - 6 =$ ____ $7 - 1 =$ ____ $5 - 1 =$ ____

Tens and Ones to 50

Write how many tens and ones.
Write the number.

1.

_2_ tens **_3_** ones = **_23_**

2.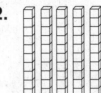

____ tens ____ ones = ____

3.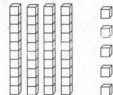

____ tens ____ ones = ____

4.

____ ten ____ ones = ____

5.

____ tens ____ ones = ____

6.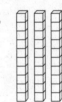

____ tens ____ one = ____

▶ **Mixed Review**

Solve.

7. $3 + 4 =$ ____ $6 + 2 =$ ____ $3 + 3 =$ ____

8. $4 + 4 =$ ____ $5 + 1 =$ ____ $4 + 2 =$ ____

9. $8 - 7 =$ ____ $5 - 2 =$ ____ $6 - 4 =$ ____

10. $8 - 3 =$ ____ $7 - 3 =$ ____ $8 - 1 =$ ____

Tens and Ones to 100

Write how many tens and ones. Write the number.

1.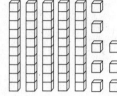

_5_ tens _8_ ones = _58_

2.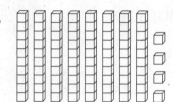

____ tens ____ ones = ____

3.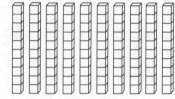

____ tens ____ ones = ____

4.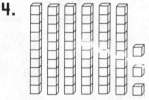

____ tens ____ ones = ____

5.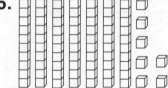

____ tens ____ ones = ____

6.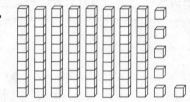

____ tens ____ ones = ____

▶ **Mixed Review**

Solve.

7. $8 + 1 =$ ____ $4 + 5 =$ ____ $3 + 6 =$ ____

8. $2 + 7 =$ ____ $3 + 5 =$ ____ $2 + 6 =$ ____

9. $9 - 1 =$ ____ $9 - 6 =$ ____ $9 - 2 =$ ____

10. $9 - 3 =$ ____ $8 - 3 =$ ____ $9 - 9 =$ ____

Expand Numbers

Write how many tens and ones.
Write the number in a different way.

1.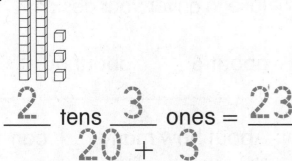

__2__ tens __3__ ones = __23__

__20__ + __3__

2.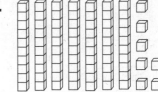

____ tens ____ ones = ____

____ + ____

3.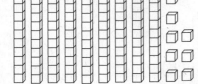

____ tens ____ ones = ____

____ + ____

4.

____ tens ____ ones = ____

____ + ____

5.

____ tens ____ ones = ____

____ + ____

6.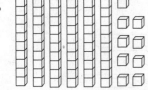

____ tens ____ one = ____

____ + ____

▶ **Mixed Review**

What comes next? Draw.

7. □ ○ □ ○ ○ □ ○ □ ○ □ ○ ____

8. △ △ ○ △ △ ○ △ △ ○ ____

Problem Solving • Make Reasonable Estimates

Circle the closer estimate.

1. About how many 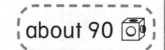 can fit in a shoe box?

   about 9 🎲   (about 90 🎲)

2. About how many does it take to cover your desk?

   about 6   about 60 📒

3. About how many 🖍 can you hold in one hand?

   about 8 🖍

   about 80 🖍

4. About how many can fit in two hands?

   about 10 🪙

   about 100

5. About how many 🎲 can you hold in one hand?

   about 5 🎲

   about 50 🎲

6. About how many small ⬭ can fit in a cup?

   about 10 ⬭

   about 100 ⬭

▶ **Mixed Review**

Solve.

7. $5 + 5 =$ _____ $10 - 7 =$ _____ $7 + 2 =$ _____

8. $5 + 3 =$ _____ $10 - 6 =$ _____ $5 + 5 =$ _____

9. $5 + 1 =$ _____ $10 - 5 =$ _____ $4 + 2 =$ _____

Greater Than

Circle the greater number.
Write the numbers.
You can use ⬚⬚⬚⬚⬚⬚⬚⬚⬚ ▭ to help.

1.   37   (73)

_73_ is greater than _37_.

_73_ > _37_

2.   93   36

_____ is greater than _____.

_____ > _____

3.   16   60

_____ is greater than _____.

_____ > _____

4.   56   59

_____ is greater than _____.

_____ > _____

5.   45   35

_____ is greater than _____.

_____ > _____

6.   19   91

_____ is greater than _____.

_____ > _____

▶ **Mixed Review**

Solve.

7. $4 + 6 =$ _____ $8 - 2 =$ _____ $3 + 5 =$ _____

8. $5 + 5 =$ _____ $4 + 5 =$ _____ $2 + 8 =$ _____

9. $9 - 2 =$ _____ $9 - 1 =$ _____ $4 + 4 =$ _____

10. $6 + 3 =$ _____ $2 + 7 =$ _____ $7 + 3 =$ _____

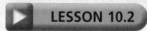

Less Than

Circle the number that is less.
Write the numbers.
You can use ⬚⬚⬚⬚⬚⬚⬚ ▢ to help.

1. (19) 61

___19___ is less than ___61___

___19___ < ___61___

2. 41 15

_____ is less than _____

_____ < _____

3. 65 56

_____ is less than _____

_____ < _____

4. 45 44

_____ is less than _____

_____ < _____

5. 13 31

_____ is less than _____

_____ < _____

6. 42 44

_____ is less than _____

_____ < _____

 Mixed Review

Solve.

7. $10 - 8 =$ ___ $10 - 7 =$ ___ $10 - 9 =$ ___

8. $10 - 4 =$ ___ $10 - 5 =$ ___ $10 - 6 =$ ___

9. $9 - 3 =$ ___ $9 - 4 =$ ___ $9 - 5 =$ ___

Name _____

Use <, =, or >

Use ⬚⬚⬚⬚⬚⬚ ▢ to show each number. Draw the ⬚⬚⬚⬚⬚⬚ ▢. Write the words and symbols.

1.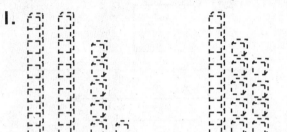

26 is greater than 19.

26 ⟩ 19

2. _____

12 is _____ 32.

12 ◯ 32

3. _____

24 is _____ 42.

24 ◯ 42

4. _____

17 is _____ 17.

17 ◯ 17

▶ **Mixed Review**

Solve.

5. $7 - 3 =$ ____ $10 - 4 =$ ____ $9 - 3 =$ ____

6. $10 - 6 =$ ____ $9 - 7 =$ ____ $8 - 3 =$ ____

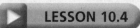

Before, After, or Between

Write the number that is between.

1.
16 | 17 | 18

2.
54 | ☐ | 56

3.
75 | ☐ | 77

4.
89 | ☐ | 91

Write the number that is just before or just after.

5.
☐ 18 19

6.
☐ 38 39

7.
29 30 ☐

8.
45 46 ☐

▶ **Mixed Review**

Solve.

9. $5 + 1 =$ _____ $8 + 2 =$ _____ $7 + 3 =$ _____

10. $10 - 3 =$ _____ $10 - 2 =$ _____ $10 - 1 =$ _____

11. $3 + 3 =$ _____ $4 + 4 =$ _____ $5 + 5 =$ _____

1 Less, 1 More

Write the numbers that are one less and one more.

	One Less		One More
1.	44	45	46
2.	___	60	___
3.	___	87	___
4.	___	23	___
5.	___	59	___
6.	___	11	___
7.	___	36	___
8.	___	98	___
9.	___	70	___

	One Less		One More
10.	___	46	___
11.	___	83	___
12.	___	19	___
13.	___	60	___
14.	___	55	___
15.	___	97	___
16.	___	78	___
17.	___	25	___
18.	___	89	___

▶ **Mixed Review**

Solve.

19. $8 + 2 =$ _____ $3 + 5 =$ _____ $4 + 3 =$ _____

20. $6 - 2 =$ _____ $8 - 1 =$ _____ $5 - 5 =$ _____

21. $9 + 1 =$ _____ $7 + 2 =$ _____ $9 + 0 =$ _____

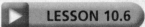

10 Less, 10 More

Write the numbers that are ten less and ten more.

	Ten Less		Ten More
1.	6	16	26
2.	___	84	___
3.	___	56	___
4.	___	41	___
5.	___	49	___
6.	___	75	___
7.	___	87	___
8.	___	23	___

	Ten Less		Ten More
9.	___	45	___
10.	___	37	___
11.	___	21	___
12.	___	19	___
13.	___	66	___
14.	___	33	___
15.	___	78	___
16.	___	40	___

▶ **Mixed Review**

Circle the number that is one less.

17.	19	18	45	46	88	87
18.	28	29	15	16	58	57
19.	10	9	59	60	73	72
20.	31	32	41	40	14	15

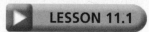

Ordinal Numbers

first   second   third   fourth   fifth   sixth   seventh   eighth   ninth   tenth

Circle to show order.

1.

first

first **red** ▷   sixth **green** ▷   ninth **yellow** ▷

2.

first

second **red** ▷   fifth **green** ▷   tenth **yellow** ▷

3.

first

third **red** ▷   fourth **blue** ▷   fifth **yellow** ▷

4.

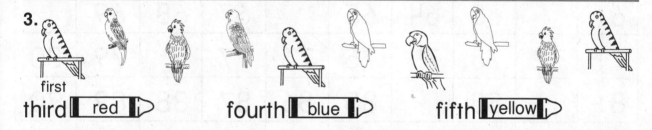

first

seventh **red** ▷   eighth **blue** ▷   ninth **green** ▷

▶ Mixed Review

Write >, <, or = in the ◯.

5. 17 ◯ 71   6. 38 ◯ 29   7. 46 ◯ 46

Patterns on a Hundred Chart

1. Write the missing numbers.
   Count by twos. Color the twos 🖊 red ▷ .
   Count by tens. Color the tens 🖊 blue ▷ .
   Some boxes will have 2 colors.

1	2	3	4	5	6	7	8	9	
11		13	14	15		17	18	19	
21	22	23	24	25	26	27		29	30
31		33	34	35		37	38	39	40
41	42	43	44	45	46	47		49	
51	52	53		55	56	57		59	60
61		63	64	65		67	68	69	
71	72	73	74	75	76	77		79	80
81		83		85	86	87	88	89	90
91		93	94	95		97		99	

▶ **Mixed Review**

Circle the greater number.

2. 28 or 18   65 or 56   89 or 98

3. 16 or 60   23 or 13   47 or 42

4. 20 or 22   79 or 76   23 or 32

Skip Count by 2s, 5s, and 10s

Skip count.
Write how many.

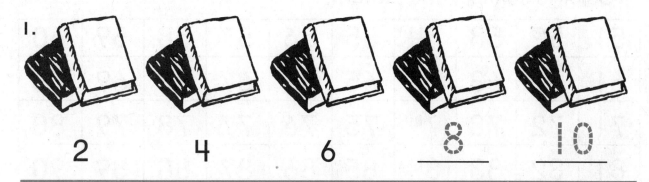

1.   2   4   6   8   10

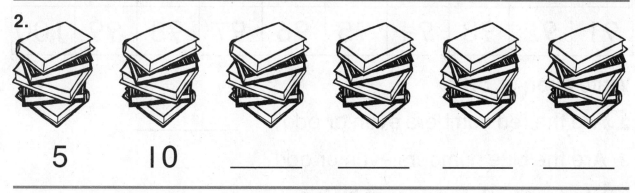

2.   5   10   ___   ___   ___   ___

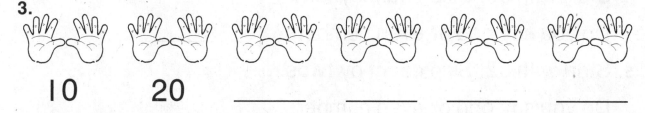

3.   10   20   ___   ___   ___   ___

▶ **Mixed Review**

Circle the number that is less.

4. 89 or 98   54 or 34   39 or 36

5. 44 or 34   83 or 92   43 or 44

6. 61 or 63   48 or 24   26 or 62

Problem Solving • Find a Pattern

1. Color 51, 53, and 55 ▎ blue ▷.
   Color 52, 54, and 56 ▎ red ▷.
   Color to continue the pattern.

51	52	53	54	55	56	57	58	59	60
61	62	63	64	65	66	67	68	69	70
71	72	73	74	75	76	77	78	79	80
81	82	83	84	85	86	87	88	89	90
91	92	93	94	95	96	97	98	99	100

Write **even** or **odd**.

2. Are the red numbers even or odd?   _____

3. Are the blue numbers even or odd?   _____

4. Start with 60. Skip count by tens.

   Do you say odd or even numbers?   _____

5. Start with 52. Skip count by twos.

   Do you say odd or even numbers?   _____

▶ **Mixed Review**

Solve.

6. $10 - 3 =$ ___ $9 - 4 =$ ___ $6 - 5 =$ ___

7. $10 - 5 =$ ___ $8 - 3 =$ ___ $7 - 2 =$ ___

8. $5 + 2 =$ ___ $4 + 4 =$ ___ $7 + 2 =$ ___

Name _____

Count On to 12

Circle the greater number.
Use the number line. Count on to add.

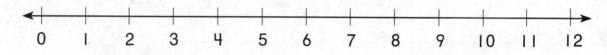

```
0   1   2   3   4   5   6   7   8   9   10   11   12
```

1.

$$
\begin{array}{r}
1 \\
+\,8 \\
\hline
9
\end{array}
\qquad
\begin{array}{r}
9 \\
+\,2 \\
\hline
\end{array}
\qquad
\begin{array}{r}
6 \\
+\,3 \\
\hline
\end{array}
\qquad
\begin{array}{r}
3 \\
+\,2 \\
\hline
\end{array}
\qquad
\begin{array}{r}
7 \\
+\,1 \\
\hline
\end{array}
$$

2.

$$
\begin{array}{r}
9 \\
+\,1 \\
\hline
\end{array}
\qquad
\begin{array}{r}
2 \\
+\,4 \\
\hline
\end{array}
\qquad
\begin{array}{r}
10 \\
+\,2 \\
\hline
\end{array}
\qquad
\begin{array}{r}
5 \\
+\,3 \\
\hline
\end{array}
\qquad
\begin{array}{r}
9 \\
+\,3 \\
\hline
\end{array}
$$

3.

$$
\begin{array}{r}
8 \\
+\,3 \\
\hline
\end{array}
\qquad
\begin{array}{r}
3 \\
+\,9 \\
\hline
\end{array}
\qquad
\begin{array}{r}
2 \\
+\,5 \\
\hline
\end{array}
\qquad
\begin{array}{r}
4 \\
+\,1 \\
\hline
\end{array}
\qquad
\begin{array}{r}
1 \\
+\,9 \\
\hline
\end{array}
$$

4.

$$
\begin{array}{r}
2 \\
+\,10 \\
\hline
\end{array}
\qquad
\begin{array}{r}
7 \\
+\,3 \\
\hline
\end{array}
\qquad
\begin{array}{r}
10 \\
+\,1 \\
\hline
\end{array}
\qquad
\begin{array}{r}
3 \\
+\,6 \\
\hline
\end{array}
\qquad
\begin{array}{r}
5 \\
+\,2 \\
\hline
\end{array}
$$

▶ **Mixed Review**

Solve.

5. $2 + 2 = $ _____ $3 + 1 = $ _____ $4 + 3 = $ _____

6. $7 - 2 = $ _____ $6 - 4 = $ _____ $8 - 4 = $ _____

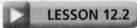

Doubles and Doubles Plus 1

Write the sum.

1. $3 + 3 =$ __6__, so $3 + 4 =$ ____.

2. $2 + 2 =$ ____, so $2 + 3 =$ ____.

3. $4 + 4 =$ ____, so $4 + 5 =$ ____.

4. $1 + 1 =$ ____, so $1 + 2 =$ ____.

5. $0 + 0 =$ ____, so $0 + 1 =$ ____.

6. $5 + 5 =$ ____, so $5 + 6 =$ ____.

Circle the doubles plus one facts. Then write the sums.

7.
$$\begin{array}{cc} 0 \\ +\ 1 \\ \hline \end{array} \quad \begin{array}{cc} 5 \\ +\ 3 \\ \hline \end{array} \quad \begin{array}{cc} 4 \\ +\ 5 \\ \hline \end{array} \quad \begin{array}{cc} 1 \\ +\ 2 \\ \hline \end{array} \quad \begin{array}{cc} 7 \\ +\ 3 \\ \hline \end{array} \quad \begin{array}{cc} 2 \\ +\ 3 \\ \hline \end{array}$$

8.
$$\begin{array}{cc} 3 \\ +\ 3 \\ \hline \end{array} \quad \begin{array}{cc} 3 \\ +\ 4 \\ \hline \end{array} \quad \begin{array}{cc} 4 \\ +\ 4 \\ \hline \end{array} \quad \begin{array}{cc} 2 \\ +\ 1 \\ \hline \end{array} \quad \begin{array}{cc} 6 \\ +\ 5 \\ \hline \end{array} \quad \begin{array}{cc} 2 \\ +\ 2 \\ \hline \end{array}$$

▶ **Mixed Review**

Solve.

9. $3 + 4 =$ ____ $2 + 3 =$ ____ $4 + 4 =$ ____

10. $9 - 4 =$ ____ $7 - 2 =$ ____ $6 - 2 =$ ____

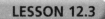

Add 3 Numbers

Circle the two numbers you add first. Write the sum.

1.

④	4	6	4	6
⑤	3	6	5	1
+ 0	+ 1	+ 0	+ 2	+ 4
9				

2.

5	3	3	2	2
3	2	4	5	3
+ 2	+ 3	+ 3	+ 5	+ 4

3.

2	3	3	1	2
1	3	5	1	5
+ 6	+ 4	+ 2	+ 6	+ 1

4.

7	4	1	7	5
3	2	3	4	2
+ 2	+ 2	+ 2	+ 1	+ 1

▶ **Mixed Review**

Solve.

5. $5 + 5 =$ _____ $8 + 3 =$ _____ $3 + 7 =$ _____

6. $6 + 5 =$ _____ $7 + 4 =$ _____ $2 + 8 =$ _____

7. $2 + 7 =$ _____ $3 + 9 =$ _____ $4 + 8 =$ _____

Name _____

LESSON 12.4

Problem Solving • Write a Number Sentence

Write a number sentence.
Draw a picture to check.

1. 9 children are at a party.
3 more children come.
How many children are at
the party now?

__9__ + __3__ = __12__ children

2. Lilly has filled two pages of
her book with stamps.
Each page has 5 stamps.
How many stamps does
she have in all?

_____ + _____ = _____ stamps

3. Amy has 9 ribbons.
May gives her 2 more ribbons.
How many ribbons does she
have in all?

_____ + _____ = _____ ribbons

4. Sam walks his dog
4 times every week.
How many times does
he walk it in two weeks?

_____ + _____ = _____ times

PW60 Practice

Name _____

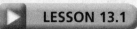

Count Back

Count back to subtract. Write the difference.
You can use the number line to help.

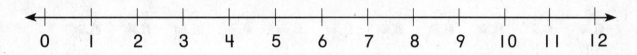

1.
$$12 - 3 = 9$$ $$9 - 3$$ $$11 - 2$$ $$7 - 2$$ $$11 - 3$$ $$12 - 2$$

2.
$$7 - 1$$ $$8 - 3$$ $$10 - 3$$ $$9 - 2$$ $$6 - 2$$ $$12 - 1$$

3.
$$11 - 1$$ $$10 - 1$$ $$8 - 2$$ $$7 - 3$$ $$10 - 2$$ $$9 - 1$$

▶ **Mixed Review**

Circle the number that is less.

4. 4 or 7	5. 8 or 10	6. 3 or 6
7. 5 or 3	8. 9 or 6	9. 8 or 9
10. 9 or 10	11. 1 or 4	12. 5 or 3

How Many More?

Draw lines to match.
Subtract to find how many more.

1.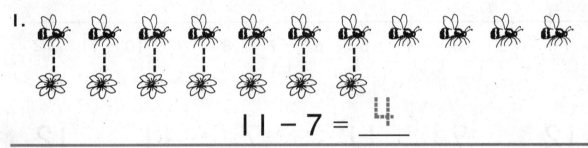

$11 - 7 =$ ____4____

2.

$10 - 8 =$ ____

3.

$11 - 9 =$ ____

4.

$12 - 8 =$ ____

▶ **Mixed Review**

Solve.

5. $5 + 4 =$ ____ $3 + 2 =$ ____ $7 - 3 =$ ____

6. $8 - 3 =$ ____ $5 + 2 =$ ____ $4 + 2 =$ ____

Related Addition and Subtraction Facts

Write the sum or difference.
Circle the related facts in each row.

1. $(4 + 3 = \underline{7})$ $3 + 3 = \underline{6}$ $(7 - 3 = \underline{4})$

2. $8 + 3 = \underline{}$ $11 - 3 = \underline{}$ $7 + 4 = \underline{}$

3. $6 + 4 = \underline{}$ $6 - 4 = \underline{}$ $10 - 4 = \underline{}$

4. $7 + 5 = \underline{}$ $3 + 9 = \underline{}$ $12 - 9 = \underline{}$

5. $4 + 8 = \underline{}$ $5 + 6 = \underline{}$ $11 - 6 = \underline{}$

6. $2 + 9 = \underline{}$ $11 - 9 = \underline{}$ $11 - 4 = \underline{}$

▶ **Mixed Review**

Solve.

7. $10 - 8 = \underline{}$ $9 + 2 = \underline{}$ $9 - 5 = \underline{}$

8. $11 - 8 = \underline{}$ $7 + 3 = \underline{}$ $7 - 2 = \underline{}$

9. $10 - 4 = \underline{}$ $8 + 2 = \underline{}$ $12 - 6 = \underline{}$

Problem Solving • Draw a Picture

Draw a picture to solve the problem.

1. Sue has 11 erasers. She gives 3 erasers to Pam. Then she gives 2 erasers to Leo. How many erasers does she have left?

   6 erasers

2. Nick has 12 tickets. He gives 6 tickets to his friends. He gives 4 tickets to his cousins. How many tickets does he have left?

   _____ tickets

3. Miss Reese has a bag of 10 apples. The children eat 5 apples. Miss Reese eats 2. How many apples are left?

   _____ apples

4. Eric draws 9 funny faces. He colors 4 faces yellow. He colors 1 face blue. How many funny faces does he have left to color?

   _____ funny faces

Use Addition to Subtract

Add. Then use the addition fact to help you subtract.

1. $6 + 4 = \underline{10}$

   $10 - 4 = \underline{6}$

2. $7 + 2 = \underline{}$

   $9 - 2 = \underline{}$

3. $5 + 6 = \underline{}$

   $11 - 6 = \underline{}$

4. $3 + 4 = \underline{}$

   $7 - 4 = \underline{}$

5. $8 + 3 = \underline{}$

   $11 - 3 = \underline{}$

6. $1 + 8 = \underline{}$

   $9 - 8 = \underline{}$

7. $3 + 7 = \underline{}$

   $10 - 7 = \underline{}$

▶ **Mixed Review**

Solve.

8. $4 + 2 + 5 = \underline{}$

9. $3 + 4 + 2 = \underline{}$

10. $8 - 3 = \underline{}$

11. $9 - 9 = \underline{}$

Fact Families

Add or subtract.
Write the numbers in the fact family.

1.

$$7 + 3 = 10 \quad 3 + 7 = 10 \quad 10 - 3 = 7 \quad 10 - 7 = 3$$

$$\boxed{7} \quad \boxed{3} \quad \boxed{10}$$

2.

$$4 + 7 \quad 7 + 4 \quad 11 - 7 \quad 11 - 4$$

$$\boxed{} \quad \boxed{} \quad \boxed{}$$

3.

$$8 + 4 \quad 4 + 8 \quad 12 - 4 \quad 12 - 8$$

$$\boxed{} \quad \boxed{} \quad \boxed{}$$

▶ **Mixed Review**

Solve.

4. $10 - 9 = $ ___

5. $8 - 4 = $ ___

6. $3 + 4 + 5 = $ ___

7. $6 + 3 + 2 = $ ___

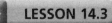

Practice Sums and Differences to 12

Add or subtract. Think of a related fact to help.

1.
$$7 + 3 = 10$$ $$5 + 5$$ $$10 - 3$$ $$10 - 5$$ $$7 + 5$$ $$12 - 5$$

2.
$$8 - 3$$ $$5 + 3$$ $$6 + 3$$ $$9 - 3$$ $$6 + 4$$ $$4 + 5$$

3.
$$5 + 6$$ $$9 - 2$$ $$10 + 2$$ $$12 - 6$$ $$8 - 4$$ $$11 - 1$$

4.
$$9 + 1$$ $$3 + 5$$ $$8 - 6$$ $$8 - 5$$ $$10 - 1$$ $$11 + 1$$

▶ **Mixed Review**

Draw a line under the pattern unit.
Then draw shapes to continue.
Complete the pattern.

5. ▭ △ ◯ ▭ △ ◯ ▭ ___ ___

6. ▭ ▭ △ ▭ ▭ △ ▭ ___ ___

Problem Solving • Choose a Strategy

Choose a different way to solve
each problem. Show your work.

1. 7 turtles swim in the pond.
Then 3 more come.
How many turtles are in
the pond?

_____10_____ turtles

2. There are 7 blue fish
and 5 red fish.
How many fish are
there in all?

_____ fish

3. There are 12 bugs.
Then 3 of them
crawl away. How
many bugs are left?

_____ bugs

4. 5 frogs jump into the pond.
Then 5 more frogs
jump into the pond.
How many frogs are
in the pond?

_____ frogs

Sort and Classify

Circle the cat that belongs in each group.

1.

2.

3.

4.

▶ **Mixed Review**

Solve.

5. $3 + 5 =$ _____ $6 - 0 =$ _____ $9 - 2 =$ _____

6. $7 + 0 =$ _____ $4 - 4 =$ _____ $2 + 3 =$ _____

7. $6 - 2 =$ _____ $7 + 2 =$ _____ $5 + 1 =$ _____

Make Tally Charts

The tally chart shows how
many there are of each toy.

Kinds of Toys	
cars	卌 l
trucks	卌

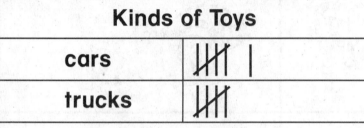

Each l stands for 1 toy.
卌 stands for 5 toys.

1. Are there fewer cars or trucks?

   _____

   _ _ _ _ _ _ _ _ _ _ _ _

   _____

2. Sort the toys another way. Make a tally chart.

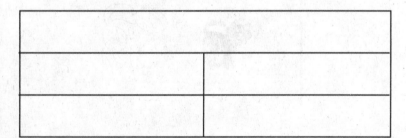

3. Write a question about your tally chart.
   Have a classmate answer your question.

   _____

   _

   _____

   _

   _____

Picture Graphs

1. Sort the toys. Draw ☺ to complete the picture graph.

Our Favorite Toys

		☺	☺	☺	☺	☺
Bears	🐻					
Cars	🚗					
Dolls	🧸					

Use the graph to answer the questions.

2. How many cars are there? _____

3. How many more bears than cars are there? _____

_____

_____

4. Are there more dolls or cars? _____

▶ **Mixed Review**

Solve.

5. $8 + 2 =$ _____ $7 + 4 =$ _____ $2 + 7 =$ _____

6. $10 - 4 =$ _____ $9 - 3 =$ _____ $8 - 5 =$ _____

Bar Graphs

Write how many tally marks there are.

Our Favorite Sports		Total
Soccer	||||| ||	7
Softball	|||||	
Football	|||	

Color the bar graph to match the tally marks.

Our Favorite Sports							
Soccer							
Softball							
Football							

0   1   2   3   4   5   6   7

Use the graph to answer
the questions.   _____

1. Which sport got 5 votes?   _____

2. Which sport did the most   _____
   children choose?
                                        _____

3. Which sport did the fewest   _____
   children choose?
                                        _____

▶ **Mixed Review**

Circle the greater number.

4. 67 or 76   28 or 22   9 or 19

Circle the number that is less.

5. 44 or 24   19 or 29   64 or 44

Problem Solving • Act it Out

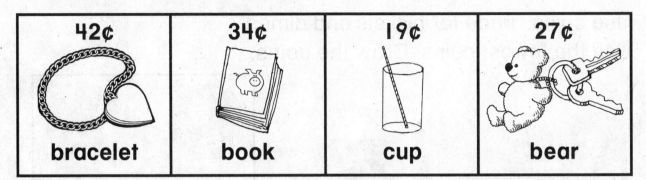

42¢	34¢	19¢	27¢
bracelet	book	cup	bear

Use pennies, nickels, and dimes to buy things.

Write what you buy. Write the amount.	Draw the coins you use to pay.
1. _____ – – – – – – – – – _____ ____¢	
2. _____ – – – – – – – – _____ ____¢	
3. _____ – – – – – – – – _____ ____¢	
4. _____ – – – – – – – _____ ____¢	

Name _____

Trade Pennies, Nickels, and Dimes

Use coins. Trade for nickels and dimes.
Use the fewest coins. Draw the coins.

1.

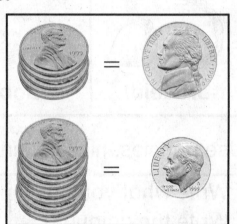

2.

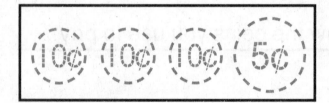

3.

▶ **Mixed Review**

Count by twos. Write the missing number.

4. 10, 12, 14, _____, 18, 20, _____, 24

5. _____, 6, 8, 10, 12, _____, 16, 18

6. 22, 24, 26, 28, _____, _____, 34, 36

Equal Amounts

Use coins.
Show the amount in two ways. Draw the coins.
Circle the way that uses fewer coins.

1.  | 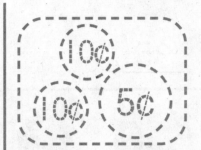 |

2.  | |

3. FARM ANIMALS 35¢ | |

▶ **Mixed Review**

Write the number that comes between.

4. 18, _____, 20

5. 29, _____, 31

6. 5, _____, 7

7. 44, _____, 46

8. 54, _____, 56

9. 36, _____, 38

Quarters

Count on from a quarter. Write the total amount.

1.

__25__ ¢, __30__ ¢, __35__ ¢   35 ¢

2.

_____ ¢, _____ ¢, _____ ¢, _____ ¢, _____ ¢   ☐ ¢

3.

_____ ¢, _____ ¢, _____ ¢, _____ ¢    ☐ ¢

▶ **Mixed Review**

Write the difference.

4. $8 - 5 =$ _____ $7 - 4 =$ _____ $6 - 4 =$ _____

5. $9 - 6 =$ _____ $8 - 0 =$ _____ $5 - 2 =$ _____

6. $7 - 5 =$ _____ $6 - 3 =$ _____ $4 - 3 =$ _____

One Dollar

Use nickels, dimes, and quarters.
Show ways to make one dollar. Draw the coins.

1.

_____

2.

_____

3.

_____

▶ **Mixed Review**

Add or subtract.

4. $5 - 3 =$ _____ $7 - 3 =$ _____ $5 + 3 =$ _____

5. $7 + 3 =$ _____ $6 - 4 =$ _____ $5 - 4 =$ _____

6. $6 + 4 =$ _____ $5 + 4 =$ _____ $4 + 2 =$ _____

7. $8 + 2 =$ _____ $8 - 2 =$ _____ $4 - 2 =$ _____

Problem Solving • Act It Out

Show the coins for each amount.
Push the coins into one group.
Draw the coins. Write the total cost.

1.

  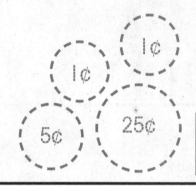

32 ¢

2.

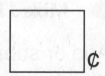 ¢

3.

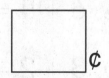 ¢

Read a Clock

Use a 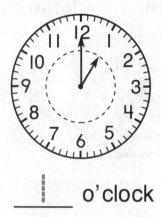. Show the time.

Write the time.

1.

_|_ o'clock

2.

_____ o'clock

3.

_____ o'clock

4.

_____ o'clock

5.
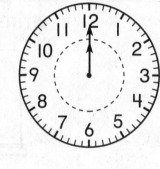

_____ o'clock

6.

_____ o'clock

▶ **Mixed Review**

Count on from a quarter. Write the total amount.

7.

_____ ¢, _____ ¢, _____ ¢, _____ ¢

☐ ¢

Problem Solving • Act it Out

About how long would it take? Circle your estimate.
Then act it out to check.

1. put 10 chairs in a circle

(more than a minute)

less than a minute

2. put a stamp on a letter

more than a minute

less than a minute

3. open a door

more than a minute

less than a minute

4. write 10 spelling words

boat
cat

more than a minute

less than a minute

5. read a big book

more than a minute

less than a minute

6. sharpen a pencil

more than a minute

less than a minute

Practice Time to the Hour and Half Hour

 Vocabulary

Draw the **hour hand** and the **minute hand.**

1.

2.

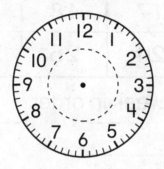

3.

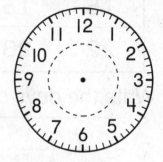

4.

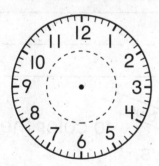

5.

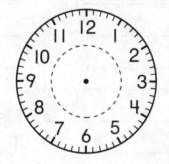

6.

 Mixed Review

Which numbers come next? Count by fives or tens.

7. 30, 40, 50, _____, _____, _____

8. 15, 20, 25, _____, _____, _____

Months and Days

FEBRUARY

Sunday	Monday	Tuesday	Wednesday	Thursday	Friday	Saturday
1	2	3	4	5	6	7
8	9	10	11	12	13	14
15	16	17	18	19	20	21
22	23	24	25	26	27	28

Write the days of the week in order.

1. Sunday _____

2. _____

3. _____

4. _____

5. _____

6. _____

7. _____

8. Use blue to color the Tuesdays.

▶ **Mixed Review**

Count on from a quarter. Write the amount.

9.

_____ ¢, _____ ¢, _____ ¢, _____ ¢, _____ ¢   ¢

Order Events

1. Draw something special you do on:

Saturday night.
Sunday morning.
Monday afternoon.

 Mixed Review

Add.

2. $4 + 3 + 1 =$ ___ $5 + 2 + 4 =$ ___ $5 + 3 + 4 =$ ___

3. $2 + 3 + 4 =$ ___ $3 + 4 + 5 =$ ___ $4 + 3 + 3 =$ ___

Problem Solving • Make a Graph

Ask 10 classmates to choose the time they most often wake up.

1. Make a tally mark for each person's choice. Then write how many.

2. Fill in the graph. First write the title. Then color the graph to match the tally marks.

Times We Wake Up		Total
6:30		
7:00		
7:30		
8:00		

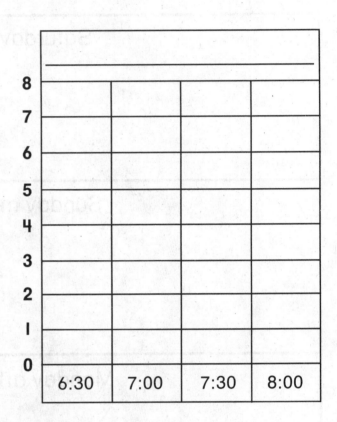

Use the graph to answer the questions.

3. At what time do the most children wake up? ____ : ____

4. At what time do the fewest children wake up? ____ : ____

5. Write a question that someone can answer by reading this graph.

_____

_____

_____

Read a Schedule

Saturday Activities	Start	End
Clean Room		
Hockey Practice		
Lunch		

Use the chart to answer the questions.

1. Which activity lasts the shortest amount of time?

   lunch

2. Which activity lasts the longest amount of time?

3. What activity is just before lunch?

▶ **Mixed Review**

Solve.

4. $4 + 4 =$ ___ $3 + 2 =$ ___ $5 + 6 =$ ___

5. $2 + 7 =$ ___ $1 + 6 =$ ___ $3 + 4 =$ ___

6. $9 + 2 =$ ___ $3 + 7 =$ ___ $3 + 5 =$ ___

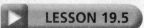

Problem Solving • Make Reasonable Estimates

Circle the closest estimate for each activity.

1.

brushing your teeth

about a week

about an hour

about a minute

2.

playing soccer

about a week

about an hour

about a minute

3.

jumping rope

about a week

about an hour

about a minute

4.

doing homework

about a week

about an hour

about a minute

5.

buying shoes

about a week

about an hour

about a minute

Solid Figures

Use solids. Compare them to the pictures.
Write the name of the solid that matches.

 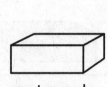 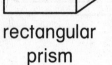   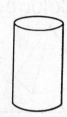

sphere   cone   rectangular prism   pyramid   cube   cylinder

1.

rectangular prism
- - - - - - - - - - - - - - -

2.

_____
- - - - - - - - - - - - - - -

3.

_____
- - - - - - - - - - - - - - -

4.

_____
- - - - - - - - - - - - - - -

5.

_____
- - - - - - - - - - - - - - -

6.

_____
- - - - - - - - - - - - - - -

Sort Solid Figures

Use solids.

1. Color each solid that will stack.

2. Color each solid that will slide.

3. Color each solid that will roll.

4. Color each solid that will roll and stack.

  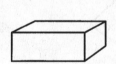

▶ **Mixed Review**

Write the missing number.

5. 77, ___, 79   44, 45, ___   ___, 32, 33

6. 56, 57, ___   88, ___, 90   ___, 91, 92

Flat Surfaces on Solids

Use solids.
Color the pictures that match the sentence.

1. This solid has 0 flat surfaces.

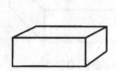

---

2. These solids have 6 flat surfaces.

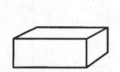

---

3. This solid has 1 flat surface.

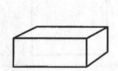

---

4. This solid has 5 flat surfaces.

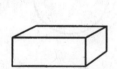

▶ **Mixed Review**

Solve.

5. $6 + 3 =$ ____ $4 + 4 =$ ____ $7 - 3 =$ ____

6. $8 - 5 =$ ____ $3 + 2 =$ ____ $6 + 2 =$ ____

Plane Shapes on Solid Figures

▶ **Vocabulary**

Color a flat **surface** to show each shape.

1.
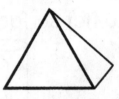

circle   square   triangle   rectangle

2. Color the triangles.

3. Color the squares.

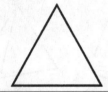

4. Color the circles.

▶ **Mixed Review**

Write + or − in the circle.

5. 2 ◯ 5 = 7   5 ◯ 3 = 2   5 ◯ 4 = 9

6. 8 ◯ 4 = 4   7 ◯ 2 = 5   6 ◯ 5 = 1

Name _____

Sort and Identify Shapes

Use 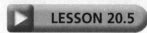 **blue** ▷ to trace each side.

Use **red** ▷ to circle each corner.

Write how many sides and corners there are.

1.

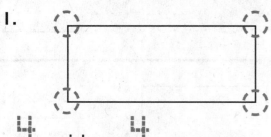

__4__ sides __4__ corners

2.

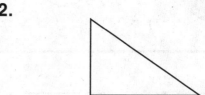

____ sides ____ corners

3.

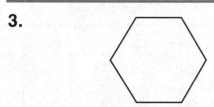

____ sides ____ corners

4.

____ sides ____ corners

5.

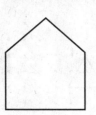

____ sides ____ corners

6.

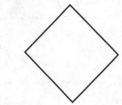

____ sides ____ corners

▶ **Mixed Review**

Circle the number that is greater.

7. 5 or 7   4 or 2   8 or 9

8. 6 or 5   1 or 7   6 or 4

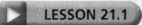

Same Size and Shape

Color the shapes that match.

1.

2.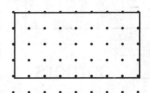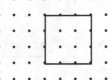

3.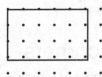

4.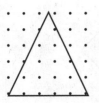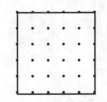

▶ **Mixed Review**

Write the sum.

5. 4 + 2 = ____   5 + 3 = ____   3 + 6 = ____

6. 4 + 3 = ____   7 + 2 = ____   3 + 2 = ____

Symmetry

Draw a line of symmetry to make two matching parts.

1.

2.
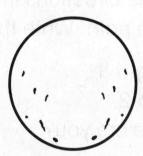

3.
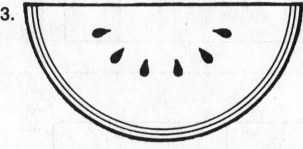

4.

5.

6.

▶ **Mixed Review**

Write the sum.

7. $2 + 4 =$ ____ $4 + 3 =$ ____ $5 + 4 =$ ____

8. $4 + 1 =$ ____ $6 + 2 =$ ____ $3 + 6 =$ ____

Give and Follow Directions

Start at ☆.
Follow the directions in order.
Draw the path. Write the name.

1. Go **right** 4.
   Go **up** 2.
   Where are you?

   _____

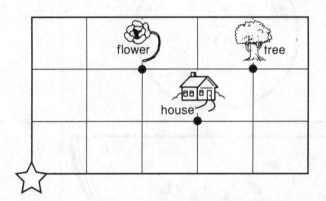

2. Go **down** 1.
   Go **left** 3.
   Go **down** 1.
   Where are you?

   _____

   _____

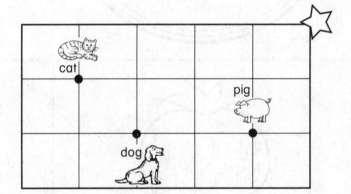

▶ **Mixed Review**

Write the difference.

3. $9 - 4 =$ _____ $5 - 4 =$ _____ $10 - 6 =$ _____

4. $7 - 3 =$ _____ $8 - 5 =$ _____ $9 - 6 =$ _____

Locate Objects

Follow the directions.

1. Color the objects just in front of the tree 〖 yellow 〗▷.

2. Color the objects just below the bench 〖 red 〗▷.

3. Color the object just behind the can 〖 brown 〗▷.

4. Draw a ball in front of the fountain.

5. Draw 3 birds above the tree.

▶ Mixed Review

Circle the greater number.

6. 9 or 8   3 or 5   2 or 3

7. 7 or 2   6 or 4   5 or 6

Problem Solving • Draw a Picture

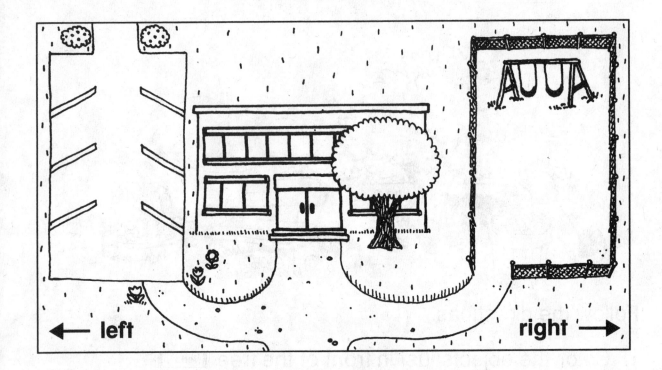

left ←   right →

Draw to complete the picture.
Follow the directions.

1. Draw a 🚗 to the left of the 🏫 .

2. Draw a 📪 to the right of the 🌳 .

3. Draw a 🚲 in front of the ⌂⌂⌂ .

4. Draw three 🌷 in front of the 🌳 .

5. Draw a 🐦 above the 🏫 .

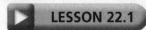
Describe and Extend Patterns

Color the R stars red .
Color the B stars blue .
Color the Y stars yellow .
Find the pattern. Then color to continue it.

1.

2.

3.

4.

 Mixed Review

Complete the doubles facts.

5. $3 + \underline{3} = \underline{6}$ $6 + \underline{} = \underline{}$ $2 + \underline{} = \underline{}$

6. $4 + \underline{} = \underline{}$ $5 + \underline{} = \underline{}$ $1 + \underline{} = \underline{}$

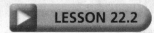

Pattern Units

Use the pictures.
Circle the pattern units.

1.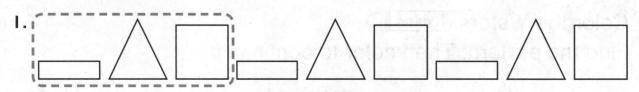

2.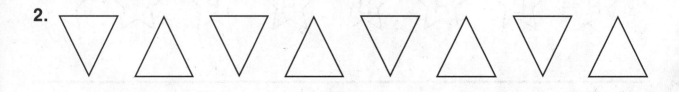

3.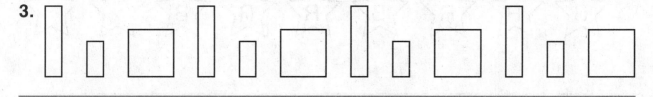

4.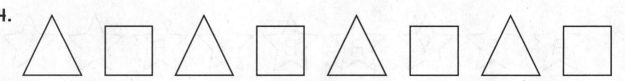

5.

▶ **Mixed Review**

Circle the number that is less.

6. 13 or 11   10 or 8   9 or 10

7. 14 or 18   3 or 5   6 or 4

Make New Patterns

Use the same shapes to make a different pattern.
Draw your new pattern.

1.

2.

3.

▶ **Mixed Review**

Write the sum.

4. $3 + 5 =$ _____ $8 + 2 =$ _____ $3 + 4 =$ _____

5. $4 + 2 =$ _____ $5 + 2 =$ _____ $2 + 2 =$ _____

Problem Solving • Find a Pattern

Use shapes to find the pattern.
Circle the mistake.

Each pattern unit is 3 shapes long.

1.

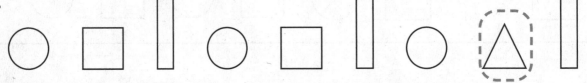

2.

3.

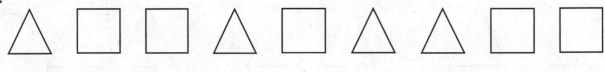

4.

5.

6.

PW106 **Practice**

Compare Lengths

Put three ▭▷ in order from shortest to longest.
Draw them. Use 🎲 to measure how long they are.

1. shortest

about _____

2.

about _____

3. longest

about _____

▶ **Mixed Review**

Solve.

4. $2 + 2 = $ ___ $4 + 4 = $ ___ $6 + 6 = $ ___

5. $3 + 3 = $ ___ $1 + 1 = $ ___ $5 + 5 = $ ___

6. $4 + 2 = $ ___ $3 + 1 = $ ___ $5 + 3 = $ ___

Use Nonstandard Units

Estimate. Then use a small to measure.

1.
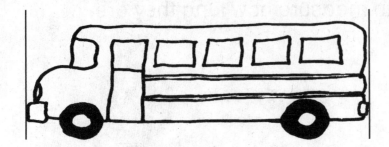

Estimate: about _____   Measure: about ___

2.

Estimate: about _____   Measure: about ___

3.

Estimate: about _____   Measure: about __

► **Mixed Review**

Solve.

4. $6 + 5 =$ ___ $11 - 4 =$ ___ $5 + 3 =$ ___

5. $12 - 4 =$ ___ $8 + 2 =$ ___ $10 - 5 =$ ___

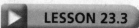
Use an Inch Ruler

Use real objects and an inch ruler.
Estimate. Then measure.

Object	Estimate	Measure
1.	about _____ inches	about _____ inches
2.	about _____ inches	about _____ inches
3.	about _____ inches	about _____ inches
4.	about _____ inches	about _____ inches

▶ **Mixed Review**

Solve.

5. $7 + 4 =$ _____ $5 + 4 =$ _____ $8 + 3 =$ _____

6. $10 - 4 =$ _____ $12 - 7 =$ _____ $11 - 5 =$ _____

Use a Centimeter Ruler

Use real objects and a centimeter ruler.
Estimate. Then measure.

Object	Estimate	Measure
1.	about _____ centimeters	about _____ centimeters
2.	about _____ centimeters	about _____ centimeters
3.	about _____ centimeters	about _____ centimeters
4.	about _____ centimeters	about _____ centimeters

► **Mixed Review**

Solve.

5. $4 + 3 =$ _____ $6 + 2 =$ _____ $7 + 5 =$ _____

6. $12 - 8 =$ _____ $10 - 2 =$ _____ $11 - 6 =$ _____

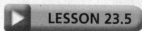

Problem Solving • Make Reasonable Estimates

Linda makes bracelets.
About how many beads long is the string?
Circle the best estimate for each bracelet.

1.

About 2   About 5   About 8

2.

About 2   About 4   About 6

3.

About 2   About 4   About 6

4.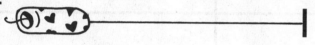

About 3   About 5   About 8

 Mixed Review

Solve.

5. $5 + 4 = $ ____ $4 + 5 = $ ____ $6 + 3 = $ ____

6. $3 + 6 = $ ____ $8 + 3 = $ ____ $3 + 8 = $ ____

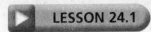

Use a Balance

Find each object and compare it to
a box of crayons.

Predict. Write **H** for heavier. Write **L** for lighter.
Then use a ⟋△⟍ to measure.

Object	Predict.	Measure.
1.	H	H
2.		
3.		
4.		
5.		

▶ **Mixed Review**

Write the sum or difference.

6. $9 - 5 =$ ___ $3 + 2 =$ ___ $8 - 6 =$ ___

7. $5 + 6 =$ ___ $12 - 9 =$ ___ $7 + 5 =$ ___

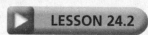

Estimate and Measure

About how many 🎲 does it take to balance?
Use real objects, a ⚖️, and 🎲.
Estimate. Then measure.

Object	Estimate.	Measure.
1.	about _____ 🎲	about _____ 🎲
2.	about _____ 🎲	about _____ 🎲
3. Crayons	about _____ 🎲	about _____ 🎲
4.	about _____ 🎲	about _____ 🎲

▶ **Mixed Review**

Circle the number that is greater.

5. 60 or 17   29 or 83   62 or 26

6. 34 or 49   15 or 50   91 or 19

7. 27 or 38   71 or 17   44 or 66

Compare Capacities

About how many cups of rice does each container hold?

Use a ⬚ and containers.

Estimate. Then measure.

Container	Estimate.	Measure.
1.	about _____ cups	about _____ cups
2.	about _____ cups	about _____ cups
3.	about _____ cups	about _____ cups
4.	about _____ cups	about _____ cups

▶ **Mixed Review**

Write the sum or difference.

5. $7 - 2 =$ ___ $6 + 3 =$ ___ $9 - 4 =$ ___

6. $12 - 5 =$ ___ $5 + 7 =$ ___ $11 - 6 =$ ___

7. $8 + 4 =$ ___ $2 + 5 =$ ___ $8 - 3 =$ ___

Problem Solving: Choose the Measuring Tool

Circle the best tool for finding each measurement.

1. Which apple is heavier?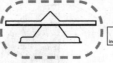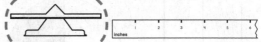

2. How tall are you?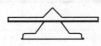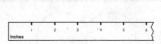

3. How wide is a book?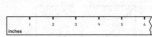

4. Which glass holds more?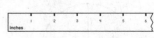

5. How much does an egg weigh?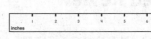

6. How much water will the sink hold?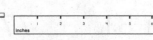

Halves

Find the shapes that show halves. Color $\frac{1}{2}$.

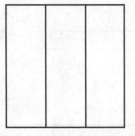 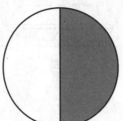 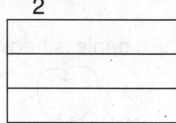

1.

 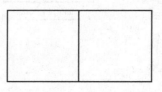 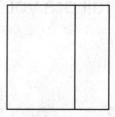

2.

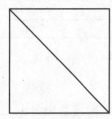 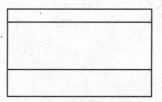 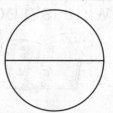

3.

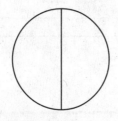  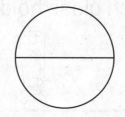

4.

▶ **Mixed Review**

Circle the number that is less.

5. 27 or 35   48 or 58   19 or 16

6. 37 or 82   71 or 67   64 or 46

7. 92 or 81   77 or 61   91 or 89

8. 23 or 63   40 or 82   54 or 45

Fourths

Color one part. Circle the fraction.

1.

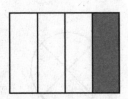

$\frac{1}{2}$ $\left(\frac{1}{4}\right)$

$\frac{1}{2}$ $\frac{1}{4}$

$\frac{1}{2}$ $\frac{1}{4}$

2.

$\frac{1}{2}$ $\frac{1}{4}$

$\frac{1}{2}$ $\frac{1}{4}$

$\frac{1}{2}$ $\frac{1}{4}$

3.

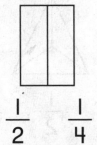

$\frac{1}{2}$ $\frac{1}{4}$

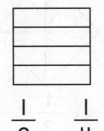

$\frac{1}{2}$ $\frac{1}{4}$

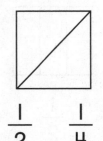

$\frac{1}{2}$ $\frac{1}{4}$

 Mixed Review

Add or subtract.

4. $3 + 5 =$ _____ $6 + 6 =$ _____ $6 + 5 =$ _____

5. $9 - 2 =$ _____ $12 - 3 =$ _____ $4 + 4 =$ _____

6. $5 + 7 =$ _____ $7 - 3 =$ _____ $11 - 4 =$ _____

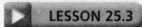

Thirds

Color one part. Circle the fraction.

1.

$\frac{1}{3}$ $\left(\frac{1}{2}\right)$ $\frac{1}{4}$

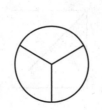

$\frac{1}{3}$ $\frac{1}{2}$ $\frac{1}{4}$

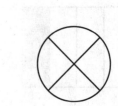

$\frac{1}{3}$ $\frac{1}{2}$ $\frac{1}{4}$

2.

$\frac{1}{3}$ $\frac{1}{2}$ $\frac{1}{4}$

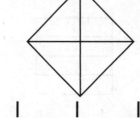

$\frac{1}{3}$ $\frac{1}{2}$ $\frac{1}{4}$

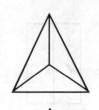

$\frac{1}{3}$ $\frac{1}{2}$ $\frac{1}{4}$

3.

$\frac{1}{3}$ $\frac{1}{2}$ $\frac{1}{4}$

$\frac{1}{3}$ $\frac{1}{2}$ $\frac{1}{4}$

$\frac{1}{3}$ $\frac{1}{2}$ $\frac{1}{4}$

▶ **Mixed Review**

Write the number that is between.

4. 45, ____, 47   74, ____, 76   41, ____, 43

5. 57, ____, 59   69, ____, 71   21, ____, 23

6. 39, ____, 41   62, ____, 64   78, ____, 80

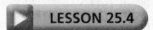

Problem Solving • Choose the Model

Think about sharing a pizza.
Circle the picture that answers the question.

1. There are 3 children. Each gets an equal share. How would you cut the pizza?

2. There are 2 children. Each gets an equal share. How would you cut the pizza?

3. There are 4 children. Each gets an equal share. Which shows one equal share?

4. There are 3 children. Each gets an equal share. Which pizza shows 3 equal parts?

5. There are 2 children. Each gets an equal share. Which shows one equal share?

Parts of Groups

Color to show each fraction.

1.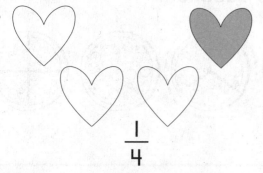

$\dfrac{1}{4}$

2.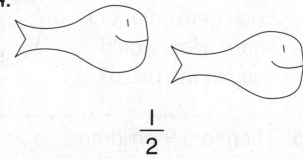

$\dfrac{1}{3}$

3.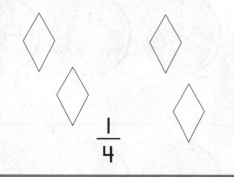

$\dfrac{1}{4}$

4.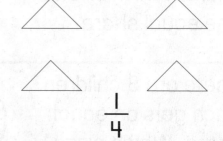

$\dfrac{1}{2}$

5.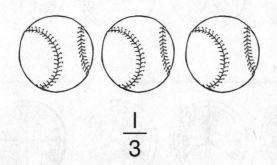

$\dfrac{1}{3}$

6.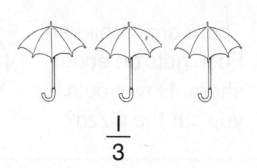

$\dfrac{1}{4}$

▶ **Mixed Review**

Write the sum or difference.

7. $3 + 4 =$ _____ $6 + 5 =$ _____ $4 + 6 =$ _____

8. $8 - 2 =$ _____ $9 - 4 =$ _____ $7 + 5 =$ _____

9. $12 - 6 =$ _____ $7 + 3 =$ _____ $11 - 4 =$ _____

Doubles and Doubles Plus 1

Write the sums.

1. $6 + 6 =$ __12__,   so $6 + 7 =$ __13__

2. $9 + 9 =$ _____,   so $9 + 10 =$ _____

3. $7 + 7 =$ _____,   so $8 + 7 =$ _____

4. $5 + 5 =$ _____,   so $5 + 6 =$ _____

5. $8 + 8 =$ _____,   so $9 + 8 =$ _____

6. $4 + 4 =$ _____,   so $5 + 4 =$ _____

Write the sums.

7.
$$\begin{array}{r} 10 \\ + 10 \\ \hline \end{array} \qquad \begin{array}{r} 6 \\ + 6 \\ \hline \end{array} \qquad \begin{array}{r} 5 \\ + 5 \\ \hline \end{array} \qquad \begin{array}{r} 8 \\ + 8 \\ \hline \end{array} \qquad \begin{array}{r} 7 \\ + 7 \\ \hline \end{array} \qquad \begin{array}{r} 9 \\ + 9 \\ \hline \end{array}$$

8.
$$\begin{array}{r} 5 \\ + 6 \\ \hline \end{array} \qquad \begin{array}{r} 8 \\ + 9 \\ \hline \end{array} \qquad \begin{array}{r} 5 \\ + 4 \\ \hline \end{array} \qquad \begin{array}{r} 10 \\ + 9 \\ \hline \end{array} \qquad \begin{array}{r} 7 \\ + 8 \\ \hline \end{array} \qquad \begin{array}{r} 6 \\ + 7 \\ \hline \end{array}$$

▶ **Mixed Review**

Add.

9. $6 + 6 =$ ___ $4 + 4 =$ ___ $2 + 2 =$ ___

10. $3 + 3 =$ ___ $1 + 1 =$ ___ $5 + 5 =$ ___

10 and More

Write the sums.

1.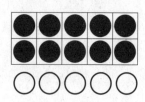

$$10 \\ +\ 3 \\ \overline{13}$$

2.

$$10 \\ +\ 8$$

3.

$$10 \\ +\ 5$$

4.

$$10 \\ +\ 7$$

5.
$$10 \\ +\ 2$$
$$6 \\ +10$$
$$10 \\ +\ 0$$
$$10 \\ +\ 4$$
$$9 \\ +10$$
$$10 \\ +\ 1$$

6.
$$5 \\ +10$$
$$10 \\ +\ 8$$
$$10 \\ +\ 9$$
$$10 \\ +\ 3$$
$$2 \\ +10$$
$$10 \\ +\ 7$$

▶ **Mixed Review**

Solve.

7. $10 - 6 = $ _____ $10 + 5 = $ _____ $10 - 5 = $ _____

8. $10 + 6 = $ _____ $10 - 7 = $ _____ $10 + 7 = $ _____

9. $8 + 8 = $ _____ $9 + 8 = $ _____ $9 - 8 = $ _____

Add 3 Numbers

Circle the numbers you add first.
Write the sum.

1. ⑦   5   2   9   1
   ⑦   5   8   2   8
  + 2   + 1   + 6   + 1   + 8
  1 6

2. 3   3   1   6   7
   3   7   6   6   5
  + 6   + 2   + 9   + 3   + 5

3. 1   7   5   8   4
   5   8   6   5   4
  + 9   + 3   + 4   + 2   + 8

▶ **Mixed Review**

Skip count. Write the missing numbers.

4. 26, 28, 30, _____, 34

5. 20, _____, 40, 50, 60

6. 55, 60, 65, _____, 75

7. 12, 14, _____, 18, 20

8. 40, 50, _____, 70, 80

9. 30, 35, 40, _____, 50

10. 25, 30, _____, 40, 45

11. 44, 46, 48, _____, 52

Problem Solving • Too Much Information

Solve. If there is extra information, cross it out.

1. Jana has 5 markers.
   Sam has 8 markers.
   ~~Jill has 2 crayons.~~
   How many markers do
   they have in all?

   __13__ markers

2. There are 6 red crayons
   and 6 blue crayons.
   How many crayons are there?

   _____ crayons

3. Tom paints 9 horses and 6 cows.
   Mike paints a truck.
   How many animals does
   Tom's paint?

   _____ animals

4. Bella has 9 dimes and 5 pennies.
   How many coins does
   Bella have?

   _____ coins

Count Back 1, 2, and 3

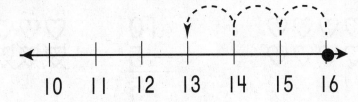

$$\begin{array}{r} 16 \\ -\ 3 \\ \hline 13 \end{array}$$

Count back to subtract. Write the difference.
Use the number line to help.

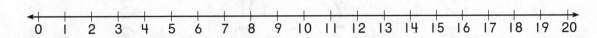

1.
$$\begin{array}{r} 10 \\ -1 \\ \hline \end{array} \quad \begin{array}{r} 19 \\ -2 \\ \hline \end{array} \quad \begin{array}{r} 11 \\ -2 \\ \hline \end{array} \quad \begin{array}{r} 14 \\ -1 \\ \hline \end{array} \quad \begin{array}{r} 17 \\ -3 \\ \hline \end{array} \quad \begin{array}{r} 20 \\ -1 \\ \hline \end{array}$$

2.
$$\begin{array}{r} 18 \\ -3 \\ \hline \end{array} \quad \begin{array}{r} 12 \\ -1 \\ \hline \end{array} \quad \begin{array}{r} 15 \\ -3 \\ \hline \end{array} \quad \begin{array}{r} 13 \\ -2 \\ \hline \end{array} \quad \begin{array}{r} 20 \\ -3 \\ \hline \end{array} \quad \begin{array}{r} 15 \\ -2 \\ \hline \end{array}$$

3.
$$\begin{array}{r} 10 \\ -2 \\ \hline \end{array} \quad \begin{array}{r} 19 \\ -3 \\ \hline \end{array} \quad \begin{array}{r} 12 \\ -2 \\ \hline \end{array} \quad \begin{array}{r} 14 \\ -3 \\ \hline \end{array} \quad \begin{array}{r} 16 \\ -1 \\ \hline \end{array} \quad \begin{array}{r} 17 \\ -2 \\ \hline \end{array}$$

▶ **Mixed Review**

Skip count. Write the missing number.

4. 20, 25, ____, 35

5. 4, 6, ____, 10

6. 28, 30, ____, 34

7. 5, 10, ____, 20

8. 30, 40, ____, 60

9. 20, 30, ____, 50

Doubles Fact Families

$$\begin{array}{r} 5 \\ + 5 \\ \hline 10 \end{array}$$

♡♡♡♡♡
♡♡♡♡♡

$$\begin{array}{r} 10 \\ - 5 \\ \hline 5 \end{array}$$

♡♡♡♡♡
✗✗✗✗✗

Add or subtract.

1.

$$\begin{array}{r} 6 \\ + 6 \\ \hline \end{array}$$ $$\begin{array}{r} 12 \\ - 6 \\ \hline \end{array}$$ $$\begin{array}{r} 7 \\ + 7 \\ \hline \end{array}$$ $$\begin{array}{r} 14 \\ - 7 \\ \hline \end{array}$$ $$\begin{array}{r} 3 \\ + 3 \\ \hline \end{array}$$ $$\begin{array}{r} 6 \\ - 3 \\ \hline \end{array}$$

2.

$$\begin{array}{r} 2 \\ + 2 \\ \hline \end{array}$$ $$\begin{array}{r} 4 \\ - 2 \\ \hline \end{array}$$ $$\begin{array}{r} 9 \\ + 9 \\ \hline \end{array}$$ $$\begin{array}{r} 18 \\ - 9 \\ \hline \end{array}$$ $$\begin{array}{r} 8 \\ + 8 \\ \hline \end{array}$$ $$\begin{array}{r} 16 \\ - 8 \\ \hline \end{array}$$

3.

$$\begin{array}{r} 8 \\ - 4 \\ \hline \end{array}$$ $$\begin{array}{r} 4 \\ + 4 \\ \hline \end{array}$$ $$\begin{array}{r} 4 \\ - 2 \\ \hline \end{array}$$ $$\begin{array}{r} 2 \\ + 2 \\ \hline \end{array}$$ $$\begin{array}{r} 10 \\ - 5 \\ \hline \end{array}$$ $$\begin{array}{r} 5 \\ + 5 \\ \hline \end{array}$$

▶ **Mixed Review**

Write the sum.

4. $9 + 6 = \underline{}$ $5 + 7 = \underline{}$ $6 + 7 = \underline{}$

5. $6 + 9 = \underline{}$ $8 + 6 = \underline{}$ $7 + 6 = \underline{}$

6. $7 + 5 = \underline{}$ $6 + 8 = \underline{}$ $9 + 9 = \underline{}$

Think Addition to Subtract

Write the sum.
Use the addition fact to help you subtract.

1.
$$\begin{array}{r} 9 \\ +9 \\ \hline 18 \end{array}$$
$$\begin{array}{r} 18 \\ -9 \\ \hline 9 \end{array}$$
$$\begin{array}{r} 8 \\ +6 \\ \hline \end{array}$$
$$\begin{array}{r} 14 \\ -6 \\ \hline \end{array}$$
$$\begin{array}{r} 6 \\ +6 \\ \hline \end{array}$$
$$\begin{array}{r} 12 \\ -6 \\ \hline \end{array}$$

2.
$$\begin{array}{r} 8 \\ +3 \\ \hline \end{array}$$
$$\begin{array}{r} 11 \\ -3 \\ \hline \end{array}$$
$$\begin{array}{r} 9 \\ +4 \\ \hline \end{array}$$
$$\begin{array}{r} 13 \\ -4 \\ \hline \end{array}$$
$$\begin{array}{r} 7 \\ +6 \\ \hline \end{array}$$
$$\begin{array}{r} 13 \\ -6 \\ \hline \end{array}$$

3.
$$\begin{array}{r} 9 \\ +7 \\ \hline \end{array}$$
$$\begin{array}{r} 16 \\ -7 \\ \hline \end{array}$$
$$\begin{array}{r} 6 \\ +5 \\ \hline \end{array}$$
$$\begin{array}{r} 11 \\ -5 \\ \hline \end{array}$$
$$\begin{array}{r} 6 \\ +8 \\ \hline \end{array}$$
$$\begin{array}{r} 14 \\ -8 \\ \hline \end{array}$$

4.
$$\begin{array}{r} 6 \\ +9 \\ \hline \end{array}$$
$$\begin{array}{r} 15 \\ -9 \\ \hline \end{array}$$
$$\begin{array}{r} 9 \\ +3 \\ \hline \end{array}$$
$$\begin{array}{r} 12 \\ -3 \\ \hline \end{array}$$
$$\begin{array}{r} 6 \\ +7 \\ \hline \end{array}$$
$$\begin{array}{r} 13 \\ -7 \\ \hline \end{array}$$

▶ **Mixed Review**

Write the sum or difference.

5. $6 + 5 = \underline{\hspace{1cm}}$ $7 + 3 = \underline{\hspace{1cm}}$ $4 + 8 = \underline{\hspace{1cm}}$

6. $11 - 6 = \underline{\hspace{1cm}}$ $10 - 7 = \underline{\hspace{1cm}}$ $12 - 4 = \underline{\hspace{1cm}}$

7. $11 - 5 = \underline{\hspace{1cm}}$ $10 - 3 = \underline{\hspace{1cm}}$ $12 - 8 = \underline{\hspace{1cm}}$

Problem Solving • Choose the Operation

Circle **add** or **subtract**.
Write the number sentence.

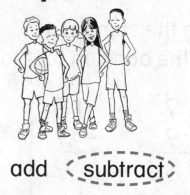

1. Jan scored 12 points.
   Hal scored 8 points.
   How many more points
   did Jan score than Hal?

   4
   _____ points

   add   ⟨subtract⟩

   12 ⊖ 8 ⊜ 4

2. Billie scored 9 points in
   the first half and 6 points
   in the second half.
   How many points is that?

   _____ points

   add   subtract

   ___ ◯ ___ ◯ ___

3. Yin scored 7 points.
   Julie scored 7 points, too.
   How many points did they
   score together?

   _____ points

   add   subtract

   ___ ◯ ___ ◯ ___

4. 13 children were playing.
   Then 5 children went home.
   How many children
   were left?

   _____ children

   add   subtract

   ___ ◯ ___ ◯ ___

Name _____

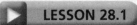

Practice Sums and Differences to 14

Add or subtract. Color each sum [green].

Color each difference [purple].

1.

$$11 - 5 = 6$$ $$6 + 7$$
$$13 - 3$$ $$7 + 7$$ $$5 + 6$$ $$11 - 8$$ $$10 - 2$$ $$9 + 4$$
$$10 - 7$$ $$10 + 3$$ $$3 + 6$$ $$14 - 7$$ $$12 - 3$$ $$8 + 3$$
$$12 - 5$$ $$7 + 3$$

▶ **Mixed Review**

Solve.

2. $1 + 2 + 7 = \_\_\_$ $2 + 4 + 4 = \_\_\_$

3. $5 + 2 + 5 = \_\_\_$ $6 + 3 + 5 = \_\_\_$

4. $3 + 6 + 3 = \_\_\_$ $6 + 2 + 4 = \_\_\_$

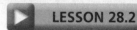

Practice Sums and Differences to 18

1. Solve the number puzzle. Write the sum or difference.
   The problems go across and down.

	7	+	10	=	17			+	7	=	
+	4					+	5			−	9
	11	−	3	=			13				6
				+							
	13				16	−	7	=			
−								+	3		
		+	8	=	12						
				−	6						
						+	8	=			

▶ **Mixed Review**

Match the related facts.

2. 10 − 7   8 + 4
   12 − 4   14 − 9
   9 + 5   7 + 3

3. 7 + 7   12 − 9
   3 + 9   14 − 7
   11 − 5   6 + 5

Practice Sums and Differences to 20

Write the sum or difference.
Color all the facts in the same family to match.

1. $\begin{array}{r} 5 \\ + 8 \\ \hline 13 \end{array}$
   red

2. $\begin{array}{r} 12 \\ - 3 \\ \hline \end{array}$
   blue

3. $\begin{array}{r} 15 \\ - 6 \\ \hline \end{array}$
   green

4. $\begin{array}{r} 9 \\ + 7 \\ \hline \end{array}$
   yellow

5. $\begin{array}{r} 7 \\ + 9 \\ \hline \end{array}$

6. $\begin{array}{r} 12 \\ - 9 \\ \hline \end{array}$

7. $\begin{array}{r} 13 \\ - 8 \\ \hline \end{array}$

8. $\begin{array}{r} 6 \\ + 9 \\ \hline \end{array}$

9. $\begin{array}{r} 15 \\ - 9 \\ \hline \end{array}$

10. $\begin{array}{r} 9 \\ + 3 \\ \hline \end{array}$

11. $\begin{array}{r} 16 \\ - 9 \\ \hline \end{array}$

12. $\begin{array}{r} 13 \\ - 5 \\ \hline \end{array}$

13. $\begin{array}{r} 8 \\ + 5 \\ \hline \end{array}$

14. $\begin{array}{r} 9 \\ + 6 \\ \hline \end{array}$

15. $\begin{array}{r} 16 \\ - 7 \\ \hline \end{array}$

16. $\begin{array}{r} 3 \\ + 9 \\ \hline \end{array}$

▶ **Mixed Review**

Solve.

17. $11 - 7 = $ _____ $15 + 3 = $ _____ $9 + 9 = $ _____

18. $20 - 3 = $ _____ $8 + 8 = $ _____ $16 + 2 = $ _____

19. $7 + 7 = $ _____ $12 - 8 = $ _____ $19 - 4 = $ _____

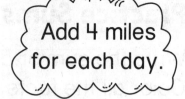

Problem Solving • Make a Table

Jen walks 4 miles each day.
How many miles does she walk in 5 days?

Add 4 miles for each day.

1. Complete the table to solve the problem.

Day	Miles Walked	Total Miles Walked
Day 1	4	4
Day 2	4	
Day 3	4	
Day 4	4	
Day 5	4	

Jen walks ____ miles in 5 days.

2. When Jen has walked 10 miles, she gives herself a sticker.
   How many days does it take her to get a sticker?

   ____ days

 Mixed Review

Find the pattern. Write the missing numbers.

3. 3, 6, 9, ___, ___, ___, 21, 24, ___, 30

4. 12, 14, 16, ___, 20, ___, ___, ___, 28, 30

5. 50, 55, 60, ___, ___, ___, 80, ___, 90, 95

6. 10, 20, 30, ___, ___, ___, 70, ___, 90, 100

Add Tens

Think:

20 + 60 means
2 tens + 6 tens.

$$\begin{array}{r} 20 \\ + 60 \\ \hline 80 \end{array}$$

$$\begin{array}{r} 2 \text{ tens} \\ + 6 \text{ tens} \\ \hline 8 \text{ tens} \end{array}$$

Use ▭▭▭▭▭ to add.

1.

$$\begin{array}{r} 10 \\ + 50 \\ \hline \end{array}$$
$$\begin{array}{r} 30 \\ + 50 \\ \hline \end{array}$$
$$\begin{array}{r} 60 \\ + 30 \\ \hline \end{array}$$
$$\begin{array}{r} 50 \\ + 20 \\ \hline \end{array}$$
$$\begin{array}{r} 20 \\ + 30 \\ \hline \end{array}$$

2.

$$\begin{array}{r} 20 \\ + 40 \\ \hline \end{array}$$
$$\begin{array}{r} 60 \\ + 10 \\ \hline \end{array}$$
$$\begin{array}{r} 30 \\ + 30 \\ \hline \end{array}$$
$$\begin{array}{r} 30 \\ + 40 \\ \hline \end{array}$$
$$\begin{array}{r} 20 \\ + 20 \\ \hline \end{array}$$

3.

$$\begin{array}{r} 40 \\ + 50 \\ \hline \end{array}$$
$$\begin{array}{r} 70 \\ + 10 \\ \hline \end{array}$$
$$\begin{array}{r} 60 \\ + 20 \\ \hline \end{array}$$
$$\begin{array}{r} 10 \\ + 80 \\ \hline \end{array}$$
$$\begin{array}{r} 20 \\ + 70 \\ \hline \end{array}$$

▶ **Mixed Review**

Write >, <, or = in the circle.

4. $5 + 4 \bigcirc 6 + 3$

5. $7 - 3 \bigcirc 6 - 1$

6. $2 + 2 \bigcirc 5 - 1$

7. $8 - 4 \bigcirc 2 + 1$

Count On by Ones

Count on to add.

Remember to start with the greater number!

1.

$3 + 50 =$ _53_

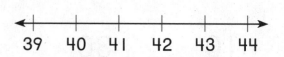

49 50 51 52 53 54 55 56

2.

9 10 11 12 13 14

$10 + 2 =$ ____

3.

39 40 41 42 43 44

$40 + 1 =$ ____

4.

19 20 21 22 23 24

$20 + 3 =$ ____

5.

59 60 61 62 63 64

$60 + 2 =$ ____

6.

69 70 71 72 73 74

$70 + 3 =$ ____

7.

29 30 31 32 33 34

$30 + 1 =$ ____

▶ **Mixed Review**

Solve.

8. $13 - 1 =$ ____ $15 -$ ____ $= 12$ $13 - 3 =$ ____

9. $14 -$ ____ $= 7$ $12 - 8 =$ ____ $16 -$ ____ $= 13$

Model Adding 1-Digit to 2-Digit Numbers

Use Workmat 3 and ▢ to add.
Make a new ten if you can.
Write the sum.

Remember:
Add the ones. Then
add the tens.

1.

Tens	Ones
2	5
+	6
3	1

Tens	Ones

2.

Tens	Ones
2	4
+	8

Tens	Ones

3.

Tens	Ones
3	8
+	7

Tens	Ones

4.

Tens	Ones
4	7
+	5

Tens	Ones

▶ **Mixed Review**

Solve.

5. $3 + 6 =$ ___ $2 + 5 =$ ___ $4 + 4 =$ ___

6. $8 - 3 =$ ___ $6 - 1 =$ ___ $4 - 4 =$ ___

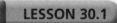

Subtract Tens

Use ⬚⬚⬚⬚⬚⬚⬚⬚ . Subtract.

Remember,
60 – 40 means
6 tens – 4 tens.

1. Think:

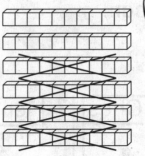

$$\begin{array}{r} 60 \\ -\ 40 \\ \hline 20 \end{array}$$

$$\begin{array}{r} 6 \text{ tens} \\ -\ 4 \text{ tens} \\ \hline 2 \text{ tens} \end{array}$$

2.
$$\begin{array}{r} 70 \\ -\ 10 \\ \hline \end{array}$$
$$\begin{array}{r} 60 \\ -\ 20 \\ \hline \end{array}$$
$$\begin{array}{r} 90 \\ -\ 70 \\ \hline \end{array}$$
$$\begin{array}{r} 80 \\ -\ 30 \\ \hline \end{array}$$
$$\begin{array}{r} 70 \\ -\ 40 \\ \hline \end{array}$$

3.
$$\begin{array}{r} 50 \\ -\ 20 \\ \hline \end{array}$$
$$\begin{array}{r} 90 \\ -\ 30 \\ \hline \end{array}$$
$$\begin{array}{r} 50 \\ -\ 10 \\ \hline \end{array}$$
$$\begin{array}{r} 20 \\ -\ 20 \\ \hline \end{array}$$
$$\begin{array}{r} 80 \\ -\ 10 \\ \hline \end{array}$$

4.
$$\begin{array}{r} 60 \\ -\ 10 \\ \hline \end{array}$$
$$\begin{array}{r} 80 \\ -\ 60 \\ \hline \end{array}$$
$$\begin{array}{r} 50 \\ -\ 40 \\ \hline \end{array}$$
$$\begin{array}{r} 30 \\ -\ 10 \\ \hline \end{array}$$
$$\begin{array}{r} 90 \\ -\ 40 \\ \hline \end{array}$$

▶ **Mixed Review**

Write the sum.

5. $6 + 6 =$ _____ $2 + 2 =$ _____ $1 + 1 =$ _____

6. $9 + 9 =$ _____ $4 + 4 =$ _____ $8 + 8 =$ _____

7. $3 + 3 =$ _____ $7 + 7 =$ _____ $5 + 5 =$ _____

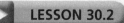

Count back by Ones

Count back to subtract.

1.

$80 - 3 =$ ___77___

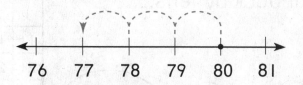

76 77 78 79 80 81

2.

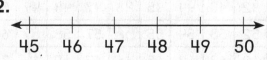

45 46 47 48 49 50

$50 - 3 =$ ___

3.

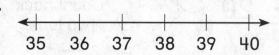

35 36 37 38 39 40

$40 - 2 =$ ___

4.

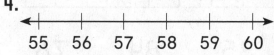

55 56 57 58 59 60

$60 - 1 =$ ___

5.

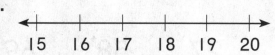

15 16 17 18 19 20

$20 - 1 =$ ___

6.

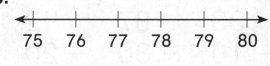

75 76 77 78 79 80

$80 - 2 =$ ___

7.

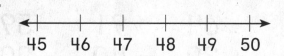

45 46 47 48 49 50

$50 - 2 =$ ___

 Mixed Review

Write the missing number.

8. $9 -$ ___ $= 4$ $6 -$ ___ $= 2$

9. $8 -$ ___ $= 3$ $7 -$ ___ $= 4$

10. $6 -$ ___ $= 3$ $9 -$ ___ $= 6$

Count Back by Tens

Use the hundred chart to subtract.
Count back by tens.

1	2	3	4	5	6	7	8	9	10
11	12	13	14	15	16	17	18	19	20
21	22	23	24	25	26	27	28	29	30
31	32	33	34	35	36	37	38	39	40
41	42	43	44	45	46	47	48	49	50
51	52	53	54	55	56	57	58	59	60
61	62	63	64	65	66	67	68	69	70
71	72	73	74	75	76	77	78	79	80
81	82	83	84	85	86	87	88	89	90
91	92	93	94	95	96	97	98	99	100

1.

$$\begin{array}{r} 56 \\ -\ 20 \\ \hline 36 \end{array}$$

Start at 56. Count back two tens.

2.
$$\begin{array}{r} 27 \\ -10 \\ \hline \end{array} \quad \begin{array}{r} 58 \\ -30 \\ \hline \end{array} \quad \begin{array}{r} 69 \\ -40 \\ \hline \end{array} \quad \begin{array}{r} 35 \\ -20 \\ \hline \end{array} \quad \begin{array}{r} 84 \\ -50 \\ \hline \end{array} \quad \begin{array}{r} 76 \\ -10 \\ \hline \end{array}$$

3.
$$\begin{array}{r} 64 \\ -30 \\ \hline \end{array} \quad \begin{array}{r} 91 \\ -40 \\ \hline \end{array} \quad \begin{array}{r} 59 \\ -20 \\ \hline \end{array} \quad \begin{array}{r} 33 \\ -10 \\ \hline \end{array} \quad \begin{array}{r} 87 \\ -30 \\ \hline \end{array} \quad \begin{array}{r} 42 \\ -20 \\ \hline \end{array}$$

▶ **Mixed Review**

Write the number that comes next.

4. 15, 20, 25, 30, _____

5. 3, 6, 9, 12, _____

6. 4, 6, 8, 10, _____

7. 30, 40, 50, 60, _____

8. 5, 10, 15, 20, _____

9. 6, 8, 10, 12, _____

10. 12, 14, 16, 18, _____

11. 4, 8, 12, 16, _____

Name _____

Subtract Tens and Ones

Use Workmat 3 and  to subtract.
Write the difference.

Remember to subtract the ones first!

1.

Tens	Ones
2	8
−	5
2	3

Tens	Ones

2.

Tens	Ones
1	9
−	5

Tens	Ones

3.

Tens	Ones
3	5
−	2

Tens	Ones

4.

Tens	Ones
3	8
−	7

Tens	Ones

▶ **Mixed Review**

Write the sum.

5. $4 + 5 + 1 =$ ___ $3 + 7 + 1 =$ ___

6. $3 + 5 + 3 =$ ___ $6 + 1 + 4 =$ ___

7. $4 + 2 + 4 =$ ___ $2 + 4 + 2 =$ ___

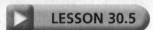

Model Subtracting 1-Digit from 2-Digit Numbers

Use Workmat 3 and ▢ to subtract.
Break apart a ten if you have to. Write the difference.

1.

tens	ones
3	4
–	5
2	9

tens	ones

2.

tens	ones
2	6
–	9

tens	ones

3.

tens	ones
4	5
–	6

tens	ones

4.

tens	ones
3	0
–	3

tens	ones

▶ **Mixed Review**

Add or Subtract.

5. $4 + 5 =$ _____ $9 - 3 =$ _____ $8 - 0 =$ _____

6. $3 + 3 =$ _____ $7 - 2 =$ _____ $8 - 1 =$ _____

7. $7 - 0 =$ _____ $5 + 5 =$ _____ $3 + 6 =$ _____

8. $11 - 3 =$ _____ $8 + 3 =$ _____ $9 - 9 =$ _____

Name _____

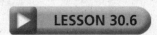
Problem Solving • Use Logical Reasoning

Ben has 13 pet mice.
Ann has 11 pet mice.
How many more mice
does Ben have?

Ben only has 13 mice, so he could not have 24 more than Ann.

(2 more)

24 more

Without adding or subtracting,
choose the reasonable answer.

1. There are 30 rabbits in the field.
   Then 20 rabbits hop away.
   How many rabbits are left?

   10 rabbits

   50 rabbits

---

2. There are 36 ants marching in a row.
   Then 12 go into a hole.
   How many ants are left?

   24 ants

   48 ants

---

3. Mary saw 50 cats on Monday.
   She saw 20 cats on Tuesday.
   How many cats did she see?

   30 cats

   70 cats

---

4. There are 27 animals in the zoo.
   There are 22 animals in the park.
   How many more animals are in the zoo?

   5 more

   49 more

---

5. 45 fish swim together in the water.
   Then 15 fish join them.
   How many fish swim together now?

   30 fish

   60 fish

Problem Solving • Use Logical Reasoning

Ben has 18 pet mice.
Ann has 41 pet mice.
How many more mice
does Ben have?

24 more

Ben only has 18 mice, so he could not have 41 more than Ann.

Without adding or subtracting,
choose the reasonable answer.

1. There are 50 rabbits in the field.
Then 20 rabbits hop away.
How many rabbits are left?

70 rabbits
30 rabbits

2. There are 36 ants marching in a row.
Then 12 go into a hole.
How many ants are left?

24 ants
48 ants

3. On Monday Mary saw 50 cars.
She saw 20 cars on Tuesday.
How many cars did she see?

30 cars
70 cars

4. There are 27 animals in the zoo.
There are 22 animals in the park.
How many more animals are in the zoo?

5 more
49 more

5. 45 fish swim together in the water.
Then 15 fish join them.
How many fish swim together now?

30 fish
60 fish